TANKMASTER

A practical guide to keeping

HEALTHY FISH
IN A STABLE ENVIRONMENT

LANCE JEPSON

BARRON'S

Author

Lance Jepson has been an avid aquarist since the age of eleven. He qualified from the University of Cambridge School of Veterinary Medicine in 1989, and since then has been largely in small animal practice, where he developed his interest in exotic animal medicine and surgery. He is Honorary Lecturer in Exotic Animal Medicine at the University of Liverpool. He has lectured extensively on exotics, especially on his main interests of ornamental fish and reptiles, and has contributed to hobbyist magazines as well as several books.

First edition for the United States and Canada published by Barron's Educational Series, Inc. 2001
First published in 2001 by Interpet Publishing
Original edition © 2001 by Interpet Publishing

All inquiries should be addressed to:
Barron's Educational Series, Inc.
250 Wireless Boulevard
Hauppauge, NY 11788
http://www.barronseduc.com

International Standard Book No. 0-7641-5277-7
Library of Congress Catalog Card No. 00-111169

Printed and bound in Indonesia

9 8 7 6 5 4 3 2 1

Credits

Created and designed: Ideas into Print, New Ash Green, Kent DA3 8JD, England.

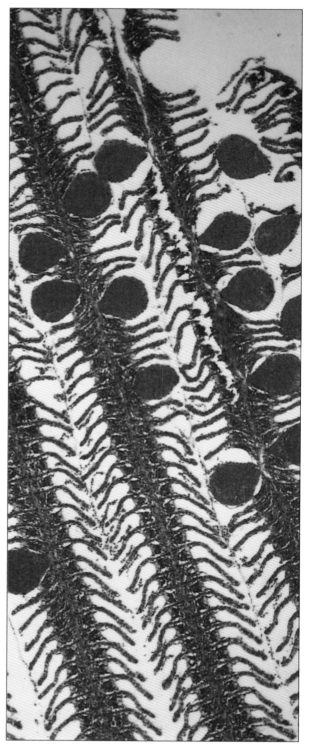

Below: This highly magnified photograph shows how chlorine damages the delicate gill tissue, causing a thickening or "clubbing" of the individual lamellae, with resultant respiratory distress.

Contents

Angelfish greedily consuming bloodworms – a picture of health and vitality.

The key to health

Introduction

The ornamental fish trade is a worldwide industry and with modern transportation techniques, literally thousands of different fish are now potentially available to today's aquarist. It is easy to forget that each of these represents a pinnacle of evolution, adapted physically and physiologically to a specific environmental niche. Failure to provide the necessary environmental conditions for any fish species will increase its susceptibility to disease and illness. Basic research on the fish we keep is therefore necessary so that we can find out what their needs are and whether we can provide them.

More than most animals kept as pets, fish are constantly in intimate contact with their immediate environment. A major part of our hobby therefore involves keeping this right, as the water in which they swim provides them with all their basic needs. These include the oxygen they need to breathe, minerals to build their skeleton, and the warmth for their body systems to function properly. It also acts as a sink for their bodily wastes, such as carbon dioxide and ammonia, which are released from the fish into the water around them. In nature, these would be immediately diluted to infinitesimal levels by the large volumes of water in which most fish are found. In the confines of an aquarium, these wastes can build up to poisonous levels unless the water quality is managed carefully.

As fishkeepers, we are in complete control of our fish's watery environment, so it is imperative that we provide the best level of water quality that we can. This is something that we can achieve only with a good working knowledge of what influences water composition, and by knowing how to apply that information.

However, as aquarists, our duties do not stop there. We must feed our fish appropriate food and keep them in an environment suitable for the expression of their normal behavior. If illness strikes, we must try to treat or alleviate their suffering. Keeping healthy fish, therefore, involves a package of skills and understanding that this book will help you to achieve.

How fish work

External anatomy

Fish are very complex organisms, with many adaptations to a completely aquatic existence. These adaptations are both physical and physiological, and a basic knowledge of these is essential for us to assess and act upon the health of the fish in our care. Here, we look at the external anatomy.

Skin

The outer surface of fish is covered by skin, which has scales embedded in it. The skin serves many functions, including:

Protection Most fish are scaled, and the scales act as protective chain mail. Many fish, such as freshwater gars (*Lepisosteus* spp.), can be very heavily scaled. Some catfish have bony plates.

Camouflage Disruptive markings or colors blending with the background can be carried by the skin.

Signaling Color changes with age (marine angelfish), sexual activity (three-spined sticklebacks – *Gasterosteus aculeatus*), or parental behavior (Texas cichlid – *Herichthys cyanoguttatus*) can be important visual signals to members of the same species, whether they are competitors for food and space, prospective sexual partners and rivals, or their own young.

Osmotic barrier It is vitally important for many physiological processes that the concentration of substances in the bloodstream, such as salts and

Osmoregulation in freshwater fish

This illustration provides an overview of how the osmotic balance is controlled in a typical freshwater fish, such as the angelfish.

The kidneys retain body salts, but remove excess water.

Water continually passes into the body through the skin and gills.

"Chloride cells" in the gills retain salts from the water flowing over them.

Some salts are lost naturally through the gills by diffusion.

Freshwater fish produces large amounts of very dilute urine.

Natural loss of water from the gills by osmosis.

Water, but not salts, absorbed in the gut.

Osmoregulation in marine fish

As part of their regulation of osmotic balance, marine fish must drink water to replace that lost from the body. This creates a salt overload that must be eliminated via the kidneys and gills.

Natural influx of salt into the gills by diffusion.

Active uptake of water by drinking seawater.

Active elimination of salts by the gills.

Small amount of urine to conserve body fluid.

Dorsal fin

Caudal fin

Anal fin

Pectoral fin (paired)

proteins, are maintained within tight limits. Fish are able to control the concentration of salts in their body by means of the kidneys and gills. These organs excrete salts if the concentration becomes too high or retain salts if the levels start to fall.

Fish skin is permeable to water molecules, which means that water can move freely from outside the fish to inside, or in the opposite direction. If we consider freshwater fish, the fluids in the tissues are more concentrated than the surrounding water. This is because blood and tissue fluids contain salts, proteins, hormones, and other natural chemicals. In an effort to "dilute" the fluids in the fish to the same concentration as the outside, water is constantly leaking into the fish. This process is called osmosis. Fortunately, intact skin acts as an osmotic barrier between the fish and the surrounding water, which means that only water molecules are able to pass through it, whereas larger molecules such as salts and proteins cannot. Such an osmotic barrier is described as a "partially permeable membrane." How fish maintain their osmotic balance is shown on page 8.

Disease barrier An intact skin dramatically reduces the opportunities for pathogens (disease-causing organisms) to invade. In addition, the mucus layer covering the surface of the skin is packed full of antibodies and other substances designed to prevent pathogens from attaching to the surface, or destroying them if they do. Even the mucus itself can be used to entrap parasites, so that when it is shed into the water, the parasites are also lost.

Pelvic fins modified into filaments

Fins

Fish possess a basic template of fins. There are two paired sets: the pectoral fins and the pelvic fins. These are used in the fine control of position. The single fins – the dorsal (top) and anal fins – help to control pitch and roll. Occasionally, a second small dorsal fin, the adipose fin, is present. The caudal (tail) fin is used for extra propulsion during swimming.

Many species of fish "ignore" this template. Freshwater pufferfish, such as Tetraodon mbu and the marine triggers (such as the Picasso trigger, Rhinecanthus aculeatus), use their dorsal and anal fins for propulsion. The small Pseudogastromyzon loaches have converted their pectoral and pelvic fins into a suction disc to resist the strong currents of their native waters.

Some species have been selectively bred for finnage variants. Those varieties with longer fins, including the double-finned goldfish varieties, are more prone to damage from trauma or infection, whereas those varieties of goldfish lacking a dorsal fin, which include the lionhead and celestial, may not be able to swim well enough to compete with normal-finned fish.

Respiration

Synchronization of mouth and opercular (gill cover) movements creates a very effective pump that draws water in through the mouth before being exhaled through the gills and between the thin flaps of gill tissue known as lamellae. These contain minute blood vessels for the uptake of oxygen and release of carbon dioxide. The gill lamellae are borne on a series of four or five gill arches on each side.

Some fish use alternative methods of breathing. The anabantids, which include the gouramis and fighting fish, have an accessory organ called the labyrinth that enables them to breathe atmospheric air. Corydoras catfish and weather loaches swallow air and they absorb oxygen across the gut wall.

The delicate gill membranes are beneath these covers.

How fish work

Virtually all the species of fish kept as ornamentals are classed as bony fish known as Teleosts, whose basic anatomical template has not changed for more than 200 million years. Here, we look in detail at the internal anatomy of a typical bony fish.

Skeleton

Fish have an internal skeleton consisting largely of a skull and backbone, with associated ribs, and bones supporting the fins. Bones in most ornamental fish contain high levels of calcium, most of which is absorbed directly from the surrounding water and the rest from food. Some fish, such as the sharks, rays, and sturgeon, have bones that are largely cartilaginous.

Muscle

The controlled contractions of muscles create the swimming movements of fish. The majority of muscles are anchored to bones, which act as a point of stability from which the muscles can exert their action. Muscles can be broadly divided into three main groups:
Cardiac, which form the beating walls of the heart.
Smooth, which form the muscular tubes of the intestines.
Skeletal. These attach to the bones. The color of these muscles depends on how well supplied they are with blood vessels.

Red muscle is well supplied with blood vessels, and is dependent on aerobic (oxygen-consuming) metabolism. These muscles are designed for

sustained use; the muscles of the pectoral fins are an example of this.

White muscle has a poor blood supply, and relies largely on anaerobic (without oxygen) metabolism. These muscles become rapidly exhausted, but are capable of short bursts of powerful activity. Instead of producing carbon dioxide like red muscle, white muscle produces lactic acid. At high levels this can be dangerous, creating a lactic acidosis that can cause death. This is thought to be the reason behind many unexplained fish deaths following excessive chasing before capture. The main propulsive muscles of the body and tail are examples of this type of muscle.

Pink muscle Some muscles, aptly called pink, are a combination of the above two types.

Circulatory system

The heart pumps blood throughout the circulatory system. As well as transporting oxygen to muscles and body organs, the red blood cells take up oxygen, before traveling straight to the gills, where the heart pumps blood

Blood circulation

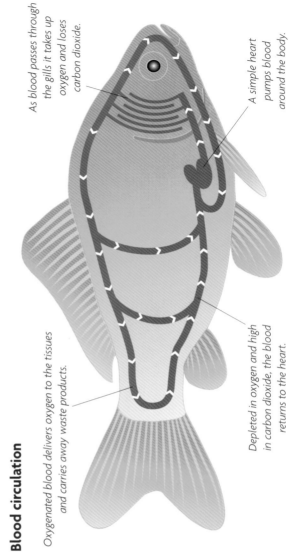

Oxygenated blood delivers oxygen to the tissues and carries away waste products.

As blood passes through the gills it takes up oxygen and loses carbon dioxide.

A simple heart pumps blood around the body.

Depleted in oxygen and high in carbon dioxide, the blood returns to the heart.

blood also carries glucose and other important substances. It also takes carbon dioxide away from those tissues. Eventually, the blood returns to the heart to repeat its journey.

Swimbladder
The swimbladder is a gas-filled organ that lies within the body cavity. It allows fish to alter their position in a water column without using valuable energy. This is achieved by altering the amount of gas in it, which in turn alters the fish's density, and how much it sinks or floats. In trout, it is a single sac, whereas in goldfish and koi, there is a cranial (front) and caudal (back) section to it; in many catfish, there are three parts to it. Some bottom-living fish, such as the cichlid *Steatocranus casuarius*, lack a swimbladder or have a severely reduced one. Goldfish varieties bred to have a spherical body, such as ryukin and orandas, have marked swimbladder abnormalities because their altered body form does not allow normal development of the swimbladder relative to the other internal organs.

Digestive system
Most fish have the basic template of a mouth armed with teeth to get hold of food, where the food is partially processed before being swallowed down to the stomach. Here acid is produced and some enzymes released to start the process of breaking down the ingested food. Once this is underway, small portions are released into the intestines, where digestion is completed and the nutritious parts are absorbed across the gut lining. Waste material is eliminated as feces.

Most fish show variations on this theme. Members of the carp family often have no teeth in the jaw. Instead, they have pharyngeal teeth in the back of the mouth that grind food against a horny pad. By taking on the job of grinding food, these teeth allow the mouth and lips to develop into an array of different structures such as suckers that allow species to radiate into different habitats. Even more extreme examples are seen in cichlids, which also possess pharyngeal teeth that have allowed evolutionary alteration of the mouth and lips into a variety of different shapes.

Some fish, such as carp and goldfish, do not possess a stomach. Other fish, particularly large predators, have very big stomachs that can expand to accommodate whole fish. Predatory fish usually have short gut lengths relative to their body length

Basic internal anatomy

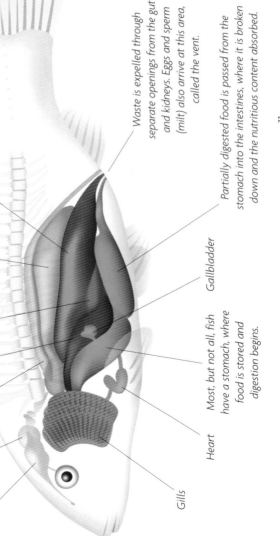

The kidneys help to control the amount of water retained in the body and play a role in immune function.

The swimbladder provides buoyancy. In most fish, the gas inside is mainly oxygen.

This is the position of the reproductive organs. The ovary and testes produce eggs and sperm (milt) respectively and these pass through a tube to the vent.

Waste is expelled through separate openings from the gut and kidneys. Eggs and sperm (milt) also arrive at this area, called the vent.

Partially digested food is passed from the stomach into the intestines, where it is broken down and the nutritious content absorbed.

Spleen

Liver

Inner ear

Brain

Gills

Heart

Most, but not all, fish have a stomach, where food is stored and digestion begins.

Gallbladder

How fish work

because animal protein is relatively easy to digest. In contrast, herbivorous fish, such as some of the loricariid sucking catfish, have very long guts in which colonies of bacteria break down much of the plant material in the diet. This process takes time, so increasing the overall length increases the time taken for food to pass through the gut.

Kidneys

In many fish, the kidney is divided into two sections. One part produces urine to excrete toxins produced within the body, and is also important in regulating salt and water balance. The other section is involved with immune function, white and red blood cell production, and antibody formation.

Liver

The liver has a great many functions, including manufacturing detoxifying substances in the body, blood proteins and blood clotting agents, as well as producing bile to help fat absorption in the intestine.

Gonads

In sexually active fish, the sex organs can be of a great size. In females, in particular, ripe ovaries can account for up to 30% of the body mass.

The endocrine system

This is the collection of glands spread throughout the body that produce and influence hormone production. It includes the pituitary gland in the brain, the gonads (source of sex hormones), and the adrenal tissue, where adrenaline, noradrenaline, and natural steroids are produced.

Nervous system

This is the collective term for the brain, spinal cord, and peripheral nerves. The brain receives and processes information from the external environment via the skin and the organs of special sense, and monitors the fish's internal body functions. Muscle movements, and ultimately, behavior are initiated by electrical impulses sent along the cranial nerves and spinal cord.

Above: Fish do not possess eyelids and cannot protect their eyes from sudden illumination. In this wreckfish (Pseudanthias squamipinnis) the color of the retina at the back of the eye has been picked out by the flash.

Below: Barbels placed at either side of the mouth of this ghost koi are well supplied with taste buds that allow the fish to taste potential food particles, such as invertebrates buried in mud, before taking them into the mouth.

Nostrils and large olfactory lobes suggest how important smell is to fish, especially as water is an ideal medium for carrying scent particles.

Large sideways-placed eyes give a maximum field of vision for detecting predators or prey. The eyeball and lens are spherical, which allows optimum vision underwater, as water is an optically dense medium.

The large optic lobes are the parts of the brain involved in interpreting the nerve signals from the eyes into the image that the fish "sees."

Sensory organs

Most fish have the five special senses of sight, hearing, smell, taste, and touch. To take full advantage of their watery environment, most species have also developed an exquisite means of detecting waves of pressure, called the lateral line. Other fish can produce and detect electrical fields in their environment.

Sight The eyes are usually large, and many fish can see in color vision. Inflammation or fluid accumulation behind one or both eyes causes them to pop out of their socket – a condition known as exophthalmia. Fish do not have eyelids, so sudden bright lights, such as switching on the lights in a darkened room, can be very stressful for them.

Hearing Fish do not possess external ears. However, many fish appear to be able to hear, often using the

Below: The lateral line appears as a series of dots that are actually small tubes in a row of scales along the flanks. The number of scales involved varies between species and this can help to distinguish closely related species.

Right: Mormyrids, such as this elephantnose (Gnathonemus petersii) possess a large brain that has evolved to interpret any changes that they detect in the electric fields that they themselves generate. It is also thought that they use electrical impulse signals to communicate with each other.

gas-filled swimbladder as a vibrating diaphragm to amplify sound waves. In carp and catfish, some of the vertebrae have been modified to form a connection between the swimbladder and the inner ear. This so-called Weberian apparatus transfers vibrations from the swimbladder wall (triggered by sound waves in the water) to the inner ear.

Smell This sense is important for many fish, not only to find food, but also to locate other members of the same species and coordinate sexual activity by detecting pheromones.

Taste Fish have a good sense of taste, and in some species, such as carp, taste buds can be found outside the mouth, allowing a fish to taste its food before it enters the mouth. The barbels of catfish are also well supplied with taste buds; indeed, in the channel catfish (*Ictalurus*), taste buds are distributed over the whole of the body surface. It is thought that these skin taste buds trigger pick-up behavior by the mouth, with the oral taste buds giving a final acceptance or rejection of the food.

Touch Fish have sensitive skin and respond to differing stimuli such as pressure, heat, cold, and pain.

Lateral line The lateral line is a specialized structure visible as a row of dots along each side of the fish. These dots are actually fluid-filled structures that respond to pressure changes in the surrounding water. They form part of an important antipredator reflex called the "C-start reflex." Here, pressure waves created by an advancing predator (or fishkeeper's net!) are detected by the lateral line on that side. This triggers an almost instantaneous contraction of the main body muscles on the other side of the fish, turning it away from the predator and triggering rapid, powerful beats of the tail to put as much distance between the fish and the predator as quickly as possible.

Electricity Some fish have developed an ability to generate electrical fields around themselves with specially adapted muscles. Most species use these for navigation, monitoring disturbances in their electrical field caused by objects around them. These fish include the mormyrids, such as the elephantnose, *Gnathonemus petersii*. The electric catfish, *Malapterurus electricus*, is able to generate large voltages very quickly. It can stun prey fish and shock potential predators, a trick it shares with the South American electric eel (*Electrophorus electricus*).

Five basic questions

Books, magazines, and the Internet provide a wealth of information on keeping ornamental fish. If you are interested in keeping particular fish, try to find out as much as possible about them before you buy. This can save a lot of suffering, heartache, and financial loss. Ask yourself these five basic questions:

How big does it grow?

Many large fish, such as the giant gourami (Osphronemus goramy) and tinfoil barbs (Barbus schwanenfeldi), are sold as small juveniles. Given the correct conditions, they rapidly grow and will soon become too big for all but the largest tanks. Also consider what you are going to keep them in. Today, aquariums and ponds are available in an enormous array of sizes, shapes, and materials. Your main

concern should be the size and shape of the pond or aquarium, which must be suitable for the eventual adult size and the number of fish you wish to keep.

Below: Osphronemus goramy grows rapidly and eventually attains a size of 40-60 cm (16-24 in). This outsize anabantid is a popular food fish throughout Asia – but accommodating it in a domestic aquarium could cause problems.

Is it compatible with other fish?

Most of the ornamental fish offered for sale are suitable for community aquariums or ponds, but many are not. Incompatibility is usually due either to territorial or predatory aggression. Territorial aggression is frequently seen in the medium-sized to larger cichlids. Another obvious example is the Siamese fighting fish (Betta splendens), where two males cannot be kept together in the average aquarium.

Predatory aggression is also often seen with the larger cichlids, such as the oscar (Astronotus ocellatus) and pike cichlids (Crenicichla spp.). Other examples are the snakeheads (Channa spp.), while in the marine aquarium, the lionfish (Pterois spp.) and groupers such as the pantherfish (Chromileptes altivelis) fall into this group. As a general rule, if a fish can fit another fish into its mouth it may try to eat it; many fish are opportunist predators and will not pass up the chance of a quick high-protein meal if it

Above: Predatory fish, such as this Channa gachua, are often sold at small sizes. As the fish grows so does its mouth, enabling it to devour larger and larger fish – which, after all, is what it is designed to do!

presents itself. This can also lead to the killing and consumption of sick fish by others in the same pond or aquarium – an excellent way of spreading diseases.

Does it like company?

Many fish are rugged individualists whose instinct is to set up and defend territories by driving away other individuals. In the wild, this reduces competition for scarce resources, such as food and egg deposition sites, but in the confines of an aquarium, it looks like merciless bullying of weaker individuals. The elephantnose (Gnathonemus petersii) is one example. On the other hand, fish such as the barbs, tetras, Corydoras catfish and the marine Chromis, are schooling fish. Their behavior and sense of well-being is tied up with a "safety-in-numbers"

14

cichlids positively thrive in hard, alkaline water, as this is what they evolved in.

What does it need to eat?

Again, most fish will do well on standard commercial fare such as flakes or pellets, but specialist feeders can cause problems. For example, seahorses (*Hippocampus* spp.) usually take only small live food such as brine shrimp and mysid shrimps, which may be difficult to provide on a daily basis. Seahorses also seem to have a high food requirement and many die, not because they lack the correct food, but because they are not given enough of it.

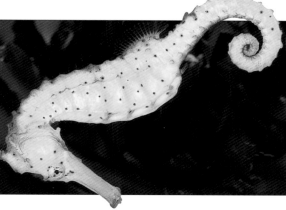

Above: Seahorses either ingest passing prey or stalk it slowly and deliberately. They cannot compete with vigorous tankmates, such as damselfish, in the confines of an aquarium.

be adjusted more closely to those of their natural environment if you wanted to breed the fish. For example, commercial strains of discus (*Symphysodon* spp.) will happily survive in water that is slightly alkaline with a moderate hardness, but will not breed unless you recreate the soft, acidic waters of their native Amazon tributaries. Cardinal tetras (*Cheirodon axelrodi*), which hail from the same environment, may well suffer long-term kidney damage if kept in hard water, as excessive mineral deposits form in their kidneys over time. Conversely, the Lake Malawi

Below: Most cardinal tetras are still wild-caught and therefore adapted to the soft waters of their birthplace. The related neon tetras have now been captive-bred commercially for so many generations that their requirement for soft water is much less than that of their wild counterparts.

Above: Keeping naturally gregarious fish such as these Chromis in numbers not only benefits the fish psychologically, but also rewards the aquarist, who is able to witness their normal schooling behavior.

mentality. Keeping them singly or in pairs will leave them feeling exposed and vulnerable to predatory attack, even if no such predators are present. Such fish can easily succumb to stress-related illnesses. As a bare minimum, keep three fish – six is better.

What water conditions does it like?

Most of the freshwater fish offered for sale will be quite happy in the water conditions found in the average aquarium or pond. These conditions can be considered suitable for maintaining many of these fish, but would need to

Temperature

The term "water quality" describes all the physical and chemical aspects of water. A basic understanding of it and how to maintain it is vital for successful long-term fishkeeping. In the following pages we look at a range of water quality parameters, starting here with temperature.

Water temperature is a critical factor in determining fish health. Fish are ectotherms, which means that they rely on the heat they absorb from their environment to drive their metabolic processes. Typically, the hobby has divided fish into two groups based on their temperature requirements, namely cold water and tropical. However, all is not as clear-cut as this simple division suggests. A more accurate classification is:

True cold water fish

There are relatively few species in this group, but it would include trout (of which a yellow albino or xanthic form is now available) and members of the sturgeon family, such as the sterlet. These are true cold water fish that are unhappy at temperatures greater than 15°C (59°F). High-latitude marines such as blennies and clingfish would also be included here.

Temperate water fish

This group includes goldfish, koi, and most other pond fish. Some aquarium fish also come under this heading, including the paradisefish (*Macropodus opercularis*), the roundtailed paradisefish (*M. ocellatus*), White Cloud Mountain minnows (*Tanichthys albonubes*), and North American sunfish (*Lepomis* spp.). These species are native to areas that

experience seasonal extremes, or that by virtue of altitude are generally cooler than their country of origin would suggest. However, many of them do enjoy higher temperatures and certainly require them for breeding. A common mistake is expecting fish in this group to thrive in what – to them – are low temperatures. Koi are the most commonly sinned against; carp enjoy temperatures of 22-28°C (72-82°F), a far cry from what they are often subjected to!

Lower temperatures

These can affect the efficiency of biological filters, as the beneficial bacteria do not function at their optimum level.

Above: *Fish may not be as "cold-blooded" as we think. Evidence suggests that carp will actively seek warmer areas or bask just beneath the pond surface in order to achieve their preferred body temperature of 22-28°C (72-82°F).*

Effects of temperature on fish health

Raising the temperature causes more of any dissolved ammonia to shift into the more toxic nonionized form (see page 18).

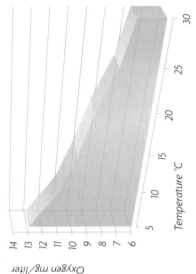

% free (toxic) ammonia in total ammonia
Temperature °C

Raising the temperature reduces the amount of dissolved oxygen present, which can cause respiratory distress.

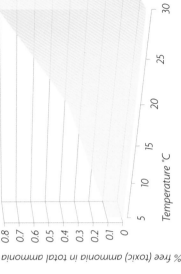

Oxygen mg/liter
Temperature °C

True tropical fish

This group includes the usual freshwater and marine tropicals offered for sale. Most enjoy a temperature range of 23-27°C (73-80°F), slightly higher for breeding. Some fish prefer even warmer conditions. Discus (*Symphysodon* spp.) and anabantids, including many of the fighting fish (*Betta* spp.) and chocolate gouramis (*Sphaerichthys osphromenoides*), are often found in slow-moving or static areas of water that can reach temperatures in the low 30s Centigrade. Aim to keep these fish at 28-30°C (82-86°F).

How does temperature affect fish?

Temperature has both direct and indirect effects on the health of fish. It has a direct effect on their metabolism. All the processes involved with the normal functioning of the fish's body, including digestion, breathing, liver and kidney function, etc., are designed to operate at their best within the temperature ranges experienced by each species of fish in its natural habitat. In species from areas where temperatures are stable all year-round, such as tropical reef fish, major fluctuations outside their normal range can rapidly have catastrophic effects on their metabolism. Other species, such as goldfish, can maintain their metabolism and survive in a much wider temperature range.

Temperature also has a direct effect on immunity. Strictly speaking, this is part of metabolism, but it is so important to the health of a fish that it deserves a separate mention. White blood cells operate best at the optimum temperature for each fish. These cells protect the fish, either by tracking down and eating invading pathogens or by producing antibodies that help to destroy them. Raising or lowering water temperature outside the preferred range for a given species can markedly depress its immune system.

Above: The White Cloud Mountain minnow is found in cool mountain streams. At true tropical temperatures, it is often more susceptible to diseases such as velvet.

Betta splendens prefers higher temperature ranges. Its ability to breathe atmospheric air is an adaptation to the hot, oxygen-deficient waters of its natural environment.

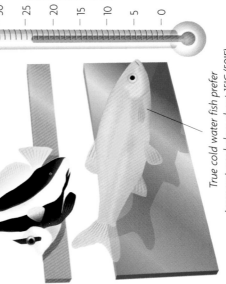

Temp in °C

True tropical fish are found within a fairly narrow temperature band of 23-30°C (73-86°F).

Temperate water fish can tolerate a much wider range of temperatures (10-25°C/50-77°F), encompassing the upper ranges of cold water fish to the mid-ranges of true tropicals – a reflection of what they experience in the wild.

A temperature range of 21-25°C (70-77°F) is suitable for most tropical marine reef fish and invertebrates.

True cold water fish prefer temperatures below about 15°C (59°F).

Temperature tolerance

Ammonia

Ammonia is the main dissolved waste product of fish and invertebrates. It is eliminated from the fish in urine and from the fish in the pond or aquarium include rotting food and fish and plant material, where it is produced by those bacteria involved in the process of decomposition. There are three measurements of ammonia that we need to be aware of.

Measuring ammonia

Total ammonia is the usual measurement of ammonia (NH_3) in a sample of water. However, when dissolved, ammonia molecules can be present in one of two forms: ionized and nonionized. Ionized ammonia (NH_4^+) is considered nontoxic, although at high concentrations it may be dangerous. Nonionized ammonia is the most dangerous form, as it can easily pass out of the bloodstream and into the brain and other organs and tissues, causing behavioral abnormalities and serious damage.

The influence of pH and temperature

The actual amount of ammonia present in one form or another depends on the temperature and pH of the water. Higher temperatures and higher pH values favor a shift toward nonionized ammonia, so more of the ammonia present will be in the more dangerous form. It is important to understand that the total ammonia level is not altered, just the relative percentage of each form.

There are many test kits that measure ammonia levels and some provide tables to convert the results to percentage ionized vs. nonionized forms.

How your aquarium matures

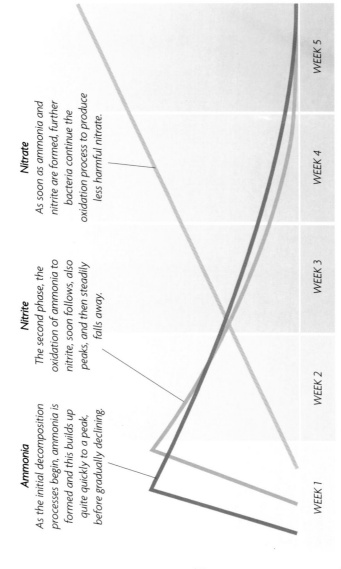

Ammonia
As the initial decomposition processes begin, ammonia is formed and this builds up quite quickly to a peak, before gradually declining.

Nitrite
The second phase, the oxidation of ammonia to nitrite, soon follows, also peaks, and then steadily falls away.

Nitrate
As soon as ammonia and nitrite are formed, further bacteria continue the oxidation process to produce less harmful nitrate.

WEEK 1   WEEK 2   WEEK 3   WEEK 4   WEEK 5

The causes of high ammonia levels

In a matured, healthy aquarium or pond, ammonia is naturally eliminated by the presence of large numbers of beneficial bacteria in the filter media and on other submerged surfaces. These bacteria, known as Nitrosomonas, feed on the ammonia and convert it to less toxic compounds called nitrites.

High ammonia levels are seen in situations where there is either an excess of ammonia production (caused by gross overfeeding and undiscovered rotting fish) or a failure to convert it to nitrite (such as filter insufficiency). This can occur as a result of sudden overstocking; increasing your stocking level from one to two fish immediately doubles the ammonia output in your system and it will take time for the *Nitrosomonas* numbers to increase to accommodate this change. An extreme example of this is "new tank syndrome," where fish are placed into a new, sterile system with no beneficial bacteria present at all. The ammonia level rapidly soars and reaches toxic levels within a day or two. Water quality tests will reveal very high ammonia levels (2.0 mg/l+) and zero nitrite and nitrate (see page 20). Be aware that certain medications and antibiotics added to the water may destroy beneficial bacterial colonies, again leading to a surge of ammonia.

The recommended ammonia level for all types of fish is less than 0.02 mg/l (ppm – parts per million). If they are rising significantly above this, consider partial water changes to dilute ammonia levels. In freshwater systems, you can add zeolite, a mineral that absorbs dissolved ammonia.

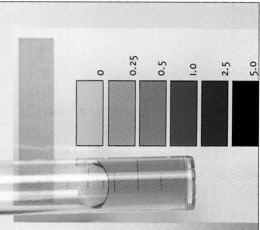

Above: A good working knowledge of water quality is essential for keeping sensitive creatures such as marine fish and invertebrates.

Left: Color change test kits, such as this one for ammonia, are suitable for the home aquarium or pond. After adding suitable reagents, the water sample will change to a color that can be read off a chart supplied with the kit.

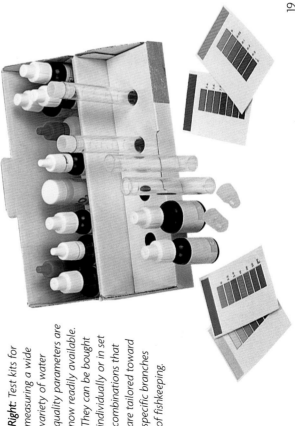

Right: Test kits for measuring a wide variety of water quality parameters are now readily available. They can be bought individually or in set combinations that are tailored toward specific branches of fishkeeping.

Nitrite

Nitrite (NO_2) is the result of *Nitrosomonas* bacteria acting upon ammonia. It is considered less toxic than ammonia, but is still very dangerous. It binds to hemoglobin, the oxygen-carrying pigment in red blood cells, so that these blood cells can no longer carry oxygen. This process cannot be reversed, so the cells become effectively useless. The hemoglobin in affected red blood cells turns from a nice healthy red to a brownish color. This can often be seen in fish that have died of nitrite toxicity, as the gills will have a dirty brown color instead of a more normal salmon pink. Affected fish gasp at the surface, desperate for oxygen, before eventually succumbing. Fish such as tiger barbs (*Barbus tetrazona tetrazona*) will adopt a headstanding position as a sign of nitrite poisoning. A nitrite level of less than 0.2 mg/l is considered safe. Levels greater than 0.5 mg/l are rapidly toxic. Continuous low-grade exposure to nitrite can cause anemia and predispose fish to secondary infections.

The causes of high nitrite levels

Nitrite is naturally eliminated by *Nitrobacter* bacteria, which "feed" on it and, in doing so, convert it to nitrate (NO_3). High nitrite levels are usually due to a failure of biological filtration. This may occur following antibiotic treatment, which lowers bacterial numbers, or as a result of exposure to low temperatures, which reduces bacterial action.

High nitrite levels are sometimes attributable to incorrect cleaning of filter media. Overzealous cleaning physically removes *Nitrobacter* bacteria from the filter media, while rinsing the media in tapwater will destroy large numbers of the bacteria because chlorine is often added to tapwater as an antibacterial agent (see page 29).

Nitrite damage on gills

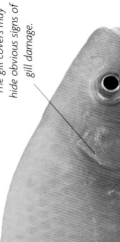

The gill covers may hide obvious signs of gill damage.

Left: Healthy gills, showing the central primary lamella with the thin-walled secondary lamellae carrying the blood vessels branching out from it.

Left: Poor water quality has damaged the delicate secondary lamellae, causing a shortening and thickening, thus reducing the surface area available.

Above: Always clean biological filter media with water from the pond or aquarium, as this will help to preserve beneficial bacterial colonies.

Above: Squeezing and rinsing out the sponge filter media will remove most of the trapped solid material but will not flush away the bacterial colonies.

Reducing high nitrite levels

High nitrite levels are best tackled by repeated partial water changes. In freshwater aquariums, adding salt to the water can be beneficial, as the chloride ions released from the salt reduce the uptake of nitrite ions by the gills. Aim for a 0.3% salt solution (use special aquarium salts or sea salt – not table salt) at 3 kg/1000 liters of pond water, or about two tablespoons (30 gm) per 10 liters of aquarium water. Note that this may damage some aquatic plants, and some fish, such as *Corydoras* catfish, may not be very salt-tolerant.

Nitrate

Nitrate (NO_3) is considered to be relatively nontoxic. In most aquariums, nitrate is the end product of ammonia elimination, and concentrations can build up over time. Nitrates can enter ponds or aquariums in the tapwater, so recommended levels are up to 50 mg/liter above ambient tapwater levels. At higher concentrations nitrate can be a stressor, predisposing fish to infections. Levels of 1600 mg/liter and above are fatal to goldfish.

The causes of high nitrate levels

There are two main causes of high nitrate levels. One is insufficient water changes; over time nitrate levels can build up to dangerous levels. The second is high tapwater levels. For most fishkeepers, this is a difficult problem to manage, particularly with sensitive fish such as discus (*Symphysodon* spp.) and marine fish. In these cases, it is a good idea to use reverse osmosis equipment. This is supplied as a module through which normal tapwater is run under pressure. The module contains a thin membrane that acts as a microscopic strainer, allowing water molecules through, but preventing larger molecules, such as nitrate, from passing across. The water that is extracted at the other end is very pure, ideal for mixing with marine salts to make high-quality artificial seawater or mimicking the natural low mineral content waters of discus.

Nitrates are utilized by aquatic plants as food, so heavily planted aquariums or ponds with growing plants will benefit. Some pondkeepers incorporate vegetable filters into their filtration systems. Regular partial water changes will control nitrate buildup.

Denitrification

Denitrification, or the conversion of nitrate to free nitrogen gas, probably occurs to a minuscule extent in most aquariums and ponds. Again, it occurs through bacterial action, but it happens in conditions of low to zero oxygen. In a marine aquarium, especially one containing invertebrates – where control of nitrate levels is crucial – this process is put to use in denitrators. Essentially, these are filtration units through which there is a very slow flow of water designed to create the dark, anoxic (oxygen-deficient) conditions in which denitrating bacteria thrive. This slow throughput limits the denitrating capability of such units, but with invertebrate aquariums, where the biological load is low, they can be a boon.

Reverse osmosis

In normal osmosis (right), water molecules pass across a partially permeable membrane from a dilute solution to a more concentrated one. With reverse osmosis, water pressure is used to reverse this flow of water molecules.

Tapwater enters the reverse osmosis unit.

A partially permeable membrane allows only water molecules through.

Pure water is drained from the unit.

Mains pressure forces water through the membrane.

Leftover water can be used on the garden.

Above: *A bed of actively growing plants situated at the filter outlet will absorb excess nitrates from the water flow before it returns to the main pond.*

21

The nitrogen cycle

The nitrogen cycle describes the sequence of conversions starting with ammonia to nitrite and then to nitrate. The nitrate is taken up by aquatic plants as a fertilizer and when fish eat the plants as food, the cycle is complete. The steps involved in the nitrogen cycle are crucial to the long-term maintenance of captive fish. In modern fishkeeping however, most of the nitrogen going into a tank or pond is in the form of flake or pelleted food, and is removed from the system largely by partial water changes.

Biological filtration

Using bacteria to remove harmful substances that are dissolved in water is known as biological filtration. There are a number of different systems available, but they all boil down to providing suitable conditions for huge colonies of the beneficial bacteria to develop. The first requirement is a substrate or surface suitable for the bacteria to colonize. This is known as the filter media and allows the bacteria to adhere and multiply on it. It is usually porous to provide maximum surface area available for colonization relative to volume.

The water flowing over the bacteria must be well oxygenated (except for denitrification, see page 21). Biological filters either have a rapid flow of water through them, constantly bathing the bacteria with oxygen-rich water, or the bacteria are exposed to atmospheric air, with only a thin layer of water keeping the media and its bacteria wet.

Other conditions for optimal bacterial activity are a pH of greater than 5.0 and relatively high temperatures of about 25-30°C (77-86°F).

The rise and fall of the nitrogen empire

Biological filters mature as the numbers of beneficial bacteria multiply to the levels needed to eliminate all of the target substance. Bear in mind that this takes time; for example, in ideal conditions it takes at least 14 days for the numbers of bacteria to respond to increased ammonia levels. At 10°C (50°F), this process can take four to eight weeks.

Bacteria can grow and multiply only if they have sufficient "food." This means that different types of bacteria develop at different rates. As a biological filter develops in a new system, the first bacteria to multiply are the "ammonia-consuming" *Nitrosomonas*, because these have plenty of "food" supplied as ammonia by the fish present. Eventually, bacterial numbers will reach a level where the exact amount of ammonia produced by the fish is used up by these bacteria. If you monitor ammonia levels, you will see a gradual rise in concentration, a leveling off and then a fall, as all the ammonia produced is used up.

As the *Nitrosomonas* bacteria "feed" on the ammonia, they produce nitrite. This encourages a gradual increase in the numbers of *Nitrobacter*, the bacteria that

Above: This pond filter uses gravel as a bacterial substrate. Water passes through an ultraviolet unit to break down suspended algae before entering the main filter. The outflow from the filter is used to create a stream back to the main pond.

Left: Power filters often use sponge as a bacterial substrate. If possible, have two filters and clean them alternately so that the biological filtration in your tank is never compromised all at once.

The nitrogen cycle

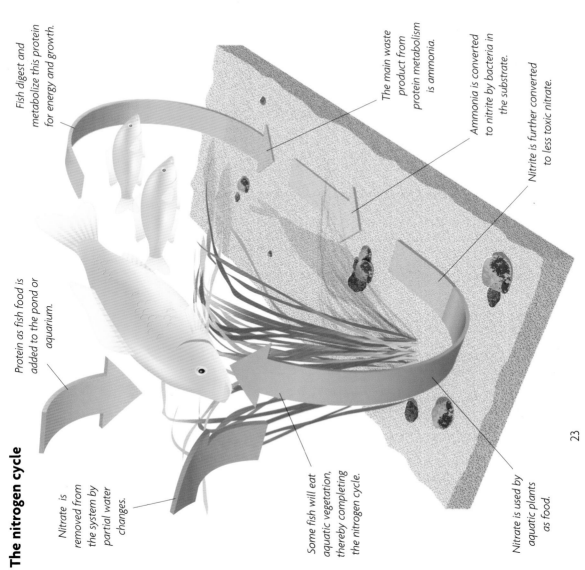

Fish digest and metabolize this protein for energy and growth.

Protein as fish food is added to the pond or aquarium.

The main waste product from protein metabolism is ammonia.

Ammonia is converted to nitrite by bacteria in the substrate.

Nitrite is further converted to less toxic nitrate.

Nitrate is removed from the system by partial water changes.

Some fish will eat aquatic vegetation, thereby completing the nitrogen cycle.

Nitrate is used by aquatic plants as food.

23

consume nitrite and produce nitrate. Thus, you will see a similar rise and fall in nitrite levels as for ammonia. The action of *Nitrobacter* bacteria causes a progressive rise in nitrate levels, which will be largely kept in check by partial water changes.

Because of this time lag in filter maturity, always stock ponds or aquariums gradually. Adding one fish to a mature aquarium containing ten equally sized fish will increase the ammonia load by 10%. But adding this same fish to a mature aquarium with only one other fish present will increase the ammonia load by 100%!

Remember that these bacteria need oxygen, too, so keep biological filters running continuously. Switching them off stops the flow of oxygenated water, creating conditions of low oxygen and a massive die-off of beneficial filter bacteria.

Below: *Regular cleaning with a gravel cleaner and siphon helps to remove excess dirt from the aquarium, and stops undergravel filter beds from compacting.*

The pH scale

The acidity of water is measured using a pH scale. The scale runs from 0.0 to 14.0. The midpoint of the pH scale is 7.0, described as neutral. Water below this (0.0-6.9) is said to be acidic, while above this (7.1-14.0) is said to be alkaline. pH is different from water hardness (see page 26), but confusion can occur because the term alkaline is occasionally used to describe hard water. In this book, alkaline will be used only to refer to water with a high pH (above 7.0).

The scale is logarithmic, so each step of one unit in the pH scale is the equivalent of a ten-fold change in water pH. For example, water at pH 6.0 is ten times more acidic than water at pH 7.0, and one hundred times (ten times ten) more acidic than at pH 8.0. Looked at another way, water at pH 8.0 is one thousand times more alkaline than at pH 5.0.

Why is the pH level important?

We need to know about pH because pH levels can have direct and indirect consequences on fish health.

Direct consequences involve the effect pH has on processes at the cellular level. Water with a low pH (acidic) can affect the ability of cells in the gills to regulate the salt balance and, as a result, the water balance of the fish. This disrupting effect can also cause a fall in blood pH (known as acidosis), which can affect cellular function throughout the body.

Right: In the enclosed environs of an aquarium, plants can have a noticeable effect on water quality. pH swings can be quite marked throughout the course of the day, especially in soft water, acidic aquariums that have very little natural buffering capacity to resist these changes.

Rapid changes in pH can be extremely stressful and affected fish may show a marked escape reaction, trying to jump out of the water or swimming frantically in an effort to find better-quality water.

Indirect effects include the shift in ammonia toward the more toxic nonionized form that is apparent with an increase in pH (i.e. becoming more alkaline). On the other hand, acidic water increases the solubility of heavy metals, such as zinc, copper, and aluminum, thus raising their toxicity.

Why do pH levels vary?

In all aquariums and ponds, there can be a buildup of organic acids released by the fish, plants, and bacteria present. Carbon dioxide is also produced by these organisms and as it dissolves in the water it produces carbonic acid that contributes to water acidity. Over time, these acids will progressively cause a fall in pH (the water becoming more acidic) and the resident fish can usually adapt to it. New fish, however, may be suddenly presented with water of a much lower pH than they are used to, with the direct consequences described above. This gradual fall in pH is particularly important in systems that should have a relatively high pH, such as marine aquariums and Rift Valley lake setups.

In some freshwater systems, carbon dioxide is pumped into the water to aid plant growth. (It is used in photosynthesis.) This gas dissolves in water, forming carbonic acid, but excessive carbon dioxide use in such setups can cause a rapid drop in pH.

Heavily planted ponds or aquariums can show extreme variations in pH during the course of the day. This is because plants and algae photosynthesize during daylight hours. As part of this process, carbon dioxide is removed from the water until eventually none is left. The result is a fall in carbonic acid levels. When this

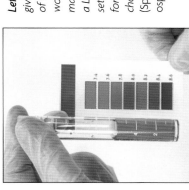

Left: This test kit is giving a pH reading of about 8.2. This would be fine for a marine aquarium or a Lake Tanganyikan setup, but disastrous for breeding chocolate gouramis (Sphaerichthys osphromenoides).

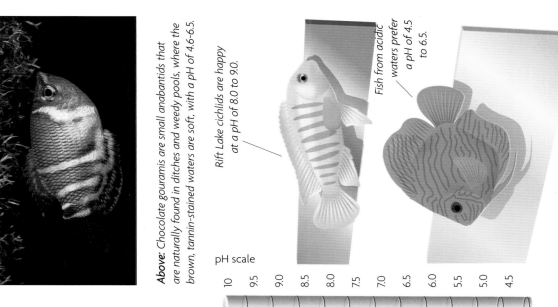

Above: Chocolate gouramis are small anabantids that are naturally found in ditches and weedy pools, where the brown, tannin-stained waters are soft, with a pH of 4.6-6.5.

pH tolerance in fish

pH scale

Rift Lake cichlids are happy at a pH of 8.0 to 9.0.

Fish from acidic waters prefer a pH of 4.5 to 6.5.

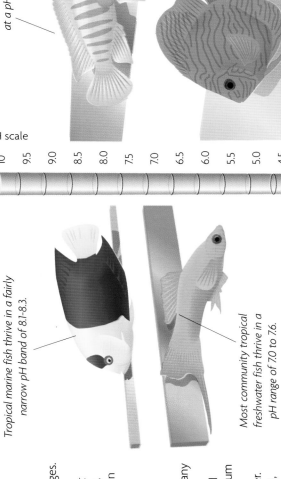

Tropical marine fish thrive in a fairly narrow pH band of 8.1-8.3.

Most community tropical freshwater fish thrive in a pH range of 7.0 to 7.6.

happens, other slightly acidic compounds, such as bicarbonate, are absorbed by the plants and algae for the same use. These processes produce an overall drop in acidity, so the pH rises.

During the hours of darkness, plants and algae do not photosynthesize but they do continue to respire. As they respire, they release carbon dioxide, which dissolves to form carbonic acid. The fish, plus the bacteria in the filtration system, are also continually producing carbon dioxide. This all combines to increase the acidity of the water, and the pH drops.

These very marked pH swings can be highly stressful to fish. To obtain meaningful results when monitoring pH in such situations, you should not only take several pH readings during the course of the day, but record when the samples were taken.

Controlling pH levels

There are three ways of controlling pH. One is by regular monitoring, plus regular partial water changes. The second method is to make use of "buffers" in high or low pH systems. These are substances that react with acidic or alkaline elements in the water, binding to them or cancelling them out to maintain the desired pH level. High pH systems, such as marine aquariums, usually contain calcium carbonate-based materials such as coral sand, dolomite, or even crushed shells, which dissolve minutely as the pH drops, effectively neutralizing any acidic effects. Synthetic seawater also contains dissolved substances that do a similar job. Low pH systems, such as discus aquariums, may use aquarium peat to maintain a low pH. This releases organic acids and tannins that continually acidify the water.

If high carbon dioxide levels are causing low pH, then vigorous aeration will allow dissolved carbon dioxide to come out of solution and escape as gas.

Hardness

Hardness is a measure of the mineral content of water. Waters with a high mineral content are termed hard, while those with low levels of dissolved minerals are described as soft. A variety of mineral compounds cause water hardness, but the one found in greatest concentrations is calcium carbonate ($CaCO_3$). Because of this, hardness usually refers to the calcium carbonate concentration, and is expressed as milligrams of calcium carbonate per liter of water (mg $CaCO_3$/l). This is also expressed as parts per million (ppm).

Why is water hardness important?

Water hardness is important for several reasons. To begin with, some fish come from naturally very soft waters, such as the Amazon tributaries. Long-term exposure of these fish to high hardness levels can trigger calcium deposits in the kidneys. Conversely, other fish are from hard water areas, such as the lakes and rivers of Central America and the Rift Valley lakes in Eastern Africa. Long-term exposure to soft water could have serious health consequences.

Once fish eggs are fertilized, they swell by absorbing water by osmosis. In soft water fish there will be a large differential in the concentration of fluids between the egg and the surrounding water, so water readily enters the egg. If these eggs are laid in hard water, this differential is reduced and less water enters the egg, which can result in a failure of the fertilized egg to develop.

Below: Placing a hard water-adapted fish such as this Placidochromis electra into a soft water system will cause it osmotic stress. The fish will use large amounts of energy just to eliminate the extra water entering it by osmosis.

Above: Lake Malawi has a pH of around 8.6 and a hardness of 250-300mg/liter. $CaCO_3$. The vast range of different species may vary with their dietary needs, but all members of this species flock require the same water conditions.

A fish in hard water

Above: Hard water has more minerals dissolved in it and is closer to the fish's own fluid concentration, so the kidneys need not work so hard to maintain the status quo. Hard water is therefore said to reduce osmotic stress.

A fish in soft water

Above: Soft water has a lower concentration of dissolved minerals, creating a greater osmotic difference between the fish and surrounding water. The gills and kidneys must work harder to eliminate the excess water that enters as a result.

Softening aquarium water

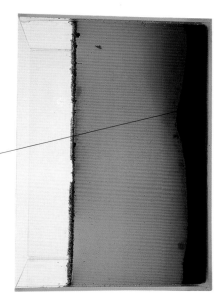

The soft substrate is beloved by many killifish and mormyrids.

1 To create a specialized aquarium for fish from soft acidic environments, use aquarium peat. Do not use garden peat; it may contain fertilizer that can be rapidly toxic to fish.

2 Gently add the peat until a 5 cm (2 in) layer covers the entire water surface. As it becomes waterlogged, the peat will slowly sink to the aquarium floor; this may take up to a week.

3 The peat gradually becomes waterlogged and the water turns brown as dissolved tannins and humic acids from the peat acidify and soften it.

Remember!

Ordinary salt does not increase water hardness – it only makes it salty! Sea salt and aquarium salts, which contain several different minerals, do affect water hardness.

Altering water hardness

Water hardness can be increased by adding crushed shells, coral sand, etc., as a source of calcium carbonate. You can reduce hardness by adding aquarium peat. In hard water, this releases humic acids that bind up the calcium present and thus reduces the hardness. Another method is to mix (virtually pure) deionized or reverse osmosis (R.O.) water with aquarium water to reduce the overall mineral content. Mixing aquarium water with the same quantity of pure water will halve the hardness.

Water hardness levels

Very soft	0 – 50 mg/l $CaCO_3$
Moderately soft	50 – 100 mg/l $CaCO_3$
Slightly hard	100 – 150 mg/l $CaCO_3$
Moderately hard	150 – 200 mg/l $CaCO_3$
Hard	200 – 300 mg/l $CaCO_3$
Very hard	300+ mg/l $CaCO_3$

Converting different scales of hardness

Although several different scales of measurement have been established in different countries, they can be easily converted with the following table.

One degree (1°) Hardness (USA) = 1.0 mg/l $CaCO_3$
One degree (1°) Clark (UK) = 143 mg/l $CaCO_3$
One degree (1°) dH (German and refers to levels of calcium oxide) = 17.9 mg/l $CaCO_3$
1 milliequivalent (meq) = 50.0 mg/l $CaCO_3$

Left: To use this test kit, dip the stick into a water sample and, after a given time interval, compare the color changes against a chart supplied.

Oxygen

Oxygen levels are very important in the aquarium. Virtually all the oxygen in a body of water gets there by dissolving into it at the surface. Oxygen is not very soluble in water, so the available levels are much lower than in atmospheric air. Recommended levels of oxygen are above 6 mg/l at 25°C (77°F) for freshwater fish and 5.5 mg/l for tropical marine fish.

The causes of reduced oxygen levels

High stocking densities play a major part in reducing oxygen levels in the aquarium, since the more fish there are, the more oxygen is consumed. Any plants in the system also use oxygen throughout the day, although during daylight hours they produce more by photosynthesis than they consume by respiration. Bear in mind that the bacteria in the biological filters are also consuming oxygen.

High temperatures and salinity are also responsible for reducing oxygen levels. Salt water holds less oxygen than fresh water, a fact to consider when stocking marine tanks. Higher altitudes reduce oxygen levels, but this is rarely a consideration. However, atmospheric pressure can be significant. Sudden fish deaths in ponds have been associated with periods of thundery weather, as low atmospheric levels trigger a fall in dissolved oxygen.

Increasing oxygen levels

Increasing movement of the water surface is an effective method of raising oxygen levels. In the aquarium, this can be achieved by bubbling air through an airstone, using submersible pumps or powerheads, or directing filter outlets at the water surface. In ponds, fountains and waterfalls perform a similar function. These mechanisms do two things: They create ripples and waves that increase the surface area available for oxygen to dissolve, and they displace oxygenated water from the surface layer, bringing deoxygenated water to the top, where it can absorb more oxygen, while the better-oxygenated water is distributed throughout the volume. Virtually no oxygen is absorbed from air bubbles pumped into ponds or aquariums; the air in them just does not stay in contact with the water long enough to dissolve.

Lowering the temperature helps to increase oxygen levels. For many marine and freshwater tropicals, a temperature of 23-25°C (73-77°F) is more than adequate for general maintenance. Lowering the salinity is another possibility. Many tropical marines will readily tolerate lower salinities, so fish-only setups can be kept at a specific gravity of 1.020 instead of the 1.023-1.025 that can be found in their native waters.

Oxygen in the water

Oxygen dissolves into the water at the surface, an effect enhanced by water movement. Carbon dioxide is released at the surface.

During daylight, carbon dioxide is absorbed by plants during photosynthesis and oxygen is released. Plants play little role in oxygenating pond or aquarium water unless present in large numbers.

Throughout the day and night, aquatic plants respire like fish, taking in oxygen and releasing carbon dioxide.

Oxygen is used up by fish. Carbon dioxide is exhaled from the gills.

Beneficial bacteria also use dissolved oxygen and release carbon dioxide into the water.

Chlorine

Chlorine, a highly reactive and poisonous gas, is added to tapwater primarily as an antibacterial agent because water companies must endeavor to produce water to certain standards for human use (so-called potable water). One of these standards sets a maximum number of bacteria present. Chlorine is not stable when dissolved, so water companies calculate the dosage such that even at the furthest point "down the line," there is still an active concentration. To improve its stability, chlorine is often combined with ammonia to form the compound chloramine. Unfortunately for fishkeepers, this has all the toxicity problems

Left: Water straight from the tap is designed for human consumption. As part of this, chlorine is added as an antibacterial agent.

about three weeks, while even minute levels of 0.002 mg/l can cause marked gill disease.

Aerating tapwater well before it is used during water changes, or leaving it to stand for 24 hours should dissipate most of the chlorine. Commercial tapwater conditioners are available. These contain sodium thiosulphate that will actively neutralize any chlorine present.

Left: When performing water changes in the aquarium using tapwater, first use a dechlorinator that removes chlorine and chloramine from tapwater (follow the directions), or allow the water to stand for 24 hours.

Below: For ponds where large volumes may make dechlorination impractical, spraying water through a hose attachment will help to disperse any chlorine before this water enters the pond.

associated with ammonia as well as chlorine.

Like ammonia, chlorine is present in two forms in solution – hypochlorous acid ($HOCl$) and hypochlorite (OCl^-) the proportion varies according to pH and temperature. The more toxic hypochlorous acid is favored by a pH level of less than 7.5 and lower temperatures. Chlorine may therefore be more hazardous in cold water aquariums or ponds. The proportion of the less toxic hypochlorite increases at pH levels greater than 7.5 and at higher temperatures.

Chlorine causes damage at the cellular level, especially affecting the gills. Constant exposure to levels normally found in tapwater can cause death in

Stocking levels

Armed with an understanding of the basics of water quality, we can now consider the application of these principles to aspects of fishkeeping.

Stocking levels

Final stocking levels are dictated by a number of factors, such as oxygen level, the efficiency of the biological filtration system, and territorial considerations.

Oxygen level depends on the surface area, temperature, and salinity of water. In most freshwater aquariums, the best way of predicting eventual stocking levels is based on surface area. Not only does this allow a minimum area for oxygen absorption per fish, but it also has built into it a space allowance for each fish. (For the stocking strategy for ponds and marine tanks, see page 31.)

Biological filtration should be such that ammonia and nitrite are eliminated as quickly as they form. Do not be guided by the apparent high stocking levels in the tanks you see in retail outlets. Their centralized filtration systems are larger and more powerful than those in domestic tanks, so that the fish are living in greater volumes of water than it seems.

The consequences of overstocking only become apparent after a water quality problem is created. However, monitoring the water quality does become an important secondary tool when assessing possible stocking densities for large fish, where aquarium size may be limiting. For example, 24 neon tetras (*Paracheirodon innesi*) each measuring 2.5 cm

Right: *When calculating the stocking densities for aquariums, estimate the length of the fish from the foremost tip of the mouth to the base of the tail. Ignore the length of the tail fin, as in this male swordtail Xiphophorus montezumae.*

Below: *A school of small tetras, such as those shown here, will create a much smaller biological load on the aquarium filtration than one large fish.*

Stocking level strategies

(1 in – not including the tail) will produce only a fraction of the waste – and consume only a fraction of the oxygen – of one 60 cm (24 in) silver arowana (*Osteoglossum bicirrhosum*).

Territorial considerations An aquarium containing ten dwarf gouramis (*Colisa lalia*) will need the same levels of dissolved oxygen and produce the same amount of biological waste as one containing ten male Siamese fighting fish (*Betta splendens*), but their behavior will be quite different! Except when breeding, *Colisa lalia* will happily coexist as a school, but male Siamese fighting fish will mercilessly attack each other until serious damage is done.

Stocking guidance

The lengths estimated for fish should not include the tail fin, so a 5 cm (2 in) swordtail (*Xiphophorus helleri*) is 5 cm (2 in) from the tip of its mouth to the base of the tail fin, not to the furthest tip of its "sword." The estimates given in the illustrations opposite are final stocking levels, which are arrived at after a number of months. Always allow at least two or three weeks between purchases to allow the biological filtration system time to "catch up."

High-oxygen fish

*Many smaller fish, such as the rosy red minnow (*Pimephales promelas*) and the hillstream loaches (Gastromyzon spp.), are inhabitants of cool, fast-flowing rivers and should be provided with a high-oxygen environment in the home aquarium.*

Pond stocking levels

2.5 cm (1 in) of fish to 45 liters (10 gallons) of pond water. This takes into account the high oxygen requirements and waste output of the often large fish kept in ponds. It also attempts to provide for minimum living space for each fish.

Tropical marine fish

Allow 2.5 cm (1 in) of fish to 18 liters (4 gallons) for the first six months, and 2.5 cm (1 in) to 9 liters (2 gallons) thereafter. Marine animals are inherently more "delicate" than their freshwater counterparts, having evolved in an incredibly stable environment. Warm salt water holds markedly less oxygen than fresh water, and the high pH levels mean that much of the ammonia produced is in the toxic, nonionized form. Many reef fish are also territorial. This stocking density attempts to take all of these variables into account.

Tropical freshwater fish

2.5 cm (1 in) of fish to 65 cm² (10 in²) of surface area. Although warmer water holds less oxygen, the relatively small size of these fish allows a higher stocking density.

Stocking level in a cold water aquarium

Allow 2.5 cm (1 in) of fish to 125 cm² (20 in²) of surface area. Temperate water is a more appropriate term for these room temperature aquariums. The lower water temperatures will hold more oxygen, but the majority of fish kept in these aquariums, such as fancy goldfish and other members of the carp family, grow relatively large and have a high oxygen demand. This stocking level should allow a safety margin for warmer periods of the year.

Routine maintenance

Routine maintenance is the key to ensuring ideal water conditions. In all cases monitor temperature on a daily basis, and ammonia, nitrite, and pH every week to two weeks. Record other parameters that you feel are appropriate. Keep a record of your results. A problem with the water quality one week ago may explain the outbreak of disease you are seeing now!

Freshwater aquariums

Carry out a partial water change every week to two weeks, using dechlorinated water at the same temperature as the aquarium water. Change 10-20% of the water at a time. Larger water changes may cause an abrupt and stressful change in water quality. Always rinse out filter media in old aquarium water, as chlorinated tapwater will destroy beneficial bacteria that may trigger an ammonia crisis.

Marine aquariums

The high cost of synthetic sea salt means that a 10-20% change every four weeks is acceptable. Rinse filter media in discarded marine water, not tapwater.

Ponds

The high rate of water loss by evaporation plus regular replenishing by rain can mean that partial water changes are generally carried out in response to a problem, not as a routine. When adding water by hose, either add a dechlorinator to the pond at the same time or spray the jet of water to allow any chlorine to dissipate. (Use a dechlorinator that removes both chlorine and chloramine.)

Pond maintenance

Keep a watch on the flow rate of water down the waterfall – a noticeable decrease may indicate that your filter needs cleaning!

Clean the biological filter regularly. Over time, the filter media will become clogged with debris, fecal material, and bacteria.

Clean and service the UV clarifier and change the tubes at regular intervals as recommended by the manufacturer.

Prune back dead or damaged leaves, as decaying plants will affect water quality. In the fall, protect against an influx of falling leaves by covering the pond with a net.

Test the water quality regularly. At the very least, check temperature, pH, ammonia, and nitrite.

During the summer in particular, evaporative water losses can be quite high. Top off regularly with dechlorinated water.

Tropical freshwater aquariums

Clean cover glasses and replace fluorescent tubes regularly to maintain lighting levels in planted tanks.

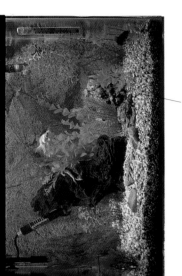

Test water quality regularly. At the very least, check temperature, pH, ammonia, and nitrite. For more delicate species, test nitrate and hardness.

Marine aquariums

Test water quality regularly. Check temperature, pH, ammonia, nitrite, and specific gravity. For more delicate species, include nitrate.

Keep looking

The secret of good animal husbandry is observation. Take the time to sit down and watch your fish (after all that's why you keep them). Are they behaving normally or is one sulking at the back? And where is that one you bought last week?

Cold water aquariums

Monitor temperature closely. Temperature affects so many important issues, such as dissolved oxygen levels, ammonia levels, appetite, and biological filter function.

Regular filter maintenance is essential.

Check pH, ammonia, and nitrite. For more delicate species include nitrate and hardness.

Cleaning the substrate regularly will reduce the amount of fish waste in the tank, thereby cutting the biological load on the filtration system.

Clean cover glasses and replace fluorescent tubes regularly to maintain lighting levels, especially in tanks housing photosynthetic invertebrates.

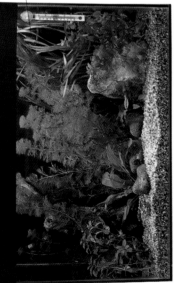

Rising specific gravity and falling water levels spell evaporative water losses. Replace this with deionized or R.O. water.

Check that all equipment such as heater/thermostats, filters, and protein skimmers are working as they should be.

Providing a healthy diet

The food you offer your fish must be of the appropriate quality and a type relevant to that species. Like all animals, fish eat to take in the calories they need to survive. Their food must contain the necessary proteins, minerals, fats, and vitamins. Generally speaking, they are better able to use fats and proteins, rather than carbohydrates, to satisfy their energy needs.

Food quality

The quality of the food describes how well it supplies the needs of the fish. High-quality food will be high in the right types of protein, not only to supply energy, but also to provide the right amino-acid balance necessary for the fish to grow and maintain itself. A food may be high in energy, but if most of this is supplied as carbohydrate, the fish may not be able to use it as well, so it would be a poor-quality food.

Fish species can be separated according to their dietary needs, and can broadly be classed as omnivores, carnivores, or herbivores.

Omnivores

Most ornamental fish fall into this category. They are opportunist feeders that take a wide variety of animal and plant-derived foods.

Carnivores

These are specialist meat-eaters and usually predatory. Many can be divided further into micropredators and macropredators. The African jewel cichlid (*Hemichromis bimaculatus*) is a

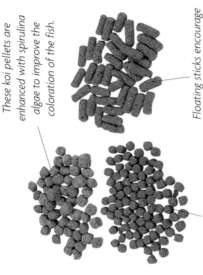

These koi pellets are enhanced with spirulina algae to improve the coloration of the fish.

High-protein pellets are ideal for pond fish in summer, when temperatures are high and protein digestion is at its best.

Floating sticks encourage fish to come to the surface. In ponds, this helps you to see the fish better and assess which ones are not feeding.

Above: *Brand name foods are nutritionally complete and should form the backbone of any feeding regime for ornamental fish, such as these koi. The nutritional needs of pond fish vary throughout the year.*

Left: *Most fish kept in the home aquarium are micropredators that feed on invertebrates found below, or taken from, the water surface. Here, a Betta pugnax has caught an insect that was trapped at the water surface.*

34

micropredator that naturally feeds on insects and fish fry. Very specialist micropredators are encountered in marine fish; for example, some of the angelfish feed exclusively on sponges.

Macropredators will take larger prey items and include fish such as the redtailed catfish (*Phractocephalus hemioliopterus*) and the clown knifefish (*Chitala ornata*). Their food should be high in protein, with relatively little fiber. You would not offer an oscar (*Astronotus ocellatus*) a lettuce leaf and expect it to be eaten. The only carbohydrate that these fish will ingest is probably in the gut of their prey.

Herbivores

There are few strictly herbivorous fish. Freshwater examples include the sucking catfish (Loricariidae), while marine fish of the tang and surgeonfish family (Acanthuridae) fall largely into this group. These fish are designed to eat relatively energy-poor plant material, and need a higher level of fiber in their diet than other species. Some of the larger sucking catfish seem to enjoy consuming driftwood – whether this supplies them with fiber or fulfills another need is not clearly understood as yet. Failure to provide this type of food results in wasting, susceptibility to disease, and eventual death.

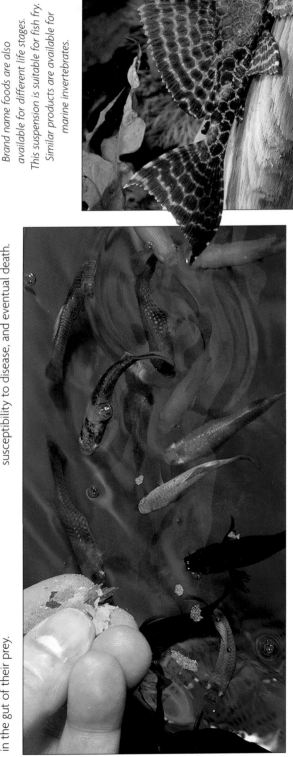

Brand name foods are also available for different life stages. This suspension is suitable for fish fry. Similar products are available for marine invertebrates.

Above: *High-quality flake foods provide a good, nutritious diet for the majority of community tropical fish. These foods are also very convenient to use and easy to store.*

Right: *Some loricariids, such as this Glyptoperichthys gibbiceps, need driftwood to rasp on. It may supply them with necessary fiber or some other dietary needs.*

Providing a healthy diet

Brand name foods

There are many brand name foods, usually supplied as flakes or pellets. Nutritionally these are sound and should form the basis of your fish's diet where possible.

Frozen foods

Usually, these consist of invertebrates, such as bloodworm or daphnia, but frozen fish such as lance fish are also available. Some other mixes contain plant material. Certain brands are gamma-irradiated. These are the preferred foods, as exposure to low-level gamma irradiation kills any intermediate parasitic stages that may be present in the food. Simple freezing may not do this. Nutritionally, these foods are close to the fresh food item, and when defrosted, the fish recognize them as food.

Dried foods

Usually, these are freeze-dried invertebrates, especially tubifex worms. This is a safe way of offering these worms, although nutritionally they may leave something to be desired. Offer them only as part of a more varied diet.

Live foods

The natural movement of live food will trigger a feeding response in all but the sickest of fish, and live foods can be used to help stimulate fish to breed. Nutritionally, they may be unbalanced (whiteworms fed to excess can cause obesity), so offer a variety of live foods in rotation to counteract this. Some wild-caught live foods, such as tubifex,

can harbor disease, so it is best to offer cultured types, such as brine shrimp.

As most ornamental fish take flake, pelleted, or frozen foods, live foods represent an unacceptable disease risk and are best avoided, unless you are keeping difficult species that need the stimulus of moving food, such as seahorses or pipefish.

Fresh foods

The supermarket can be a source of healthy fish food. Large carnivorous fish can be fed trout strips or prawns, mussels, etc. Daily offerings of leafy greens, such as lettuce, will increase the fiber intake of many herbivorous fish. Be careful, however, as such foods may rapidly foul the water and trigger a water quality crisis if not eaten or removed.

Left: Bloodworms are aquatic insect larvae, frequently available as live food. Most fish will accept them, but be aware that some people can become allergic to them and develop itchy rashes after handling them.

Dry foods

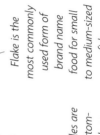

Freeze-dried mosquito larvae can be offered as part of a more varied diet.

Stick-on tablets can be used to bring fish to the front of the tank for observation.

Flake is the most commonly used form of brand name food for small to medium-sized fish.

Freeze-dried tubifex is a safe way of offering this invertebrate food.

Sinking granules are ideal for bottom-feeders, such as Corydoras catfish.

Fresh foods

Offer lettuce as a source of fiber. First scald the leaves gently to make it easier to eat.

Koi enjoy brown bread. Break it into pieces or throw a whole slice into the pond.

Colored vegetables, such as sweet corn, are a source of vitamin A.

Peas provide a source of vegetable protein for herbivores and omnivores.

Right: Before offering your fish frozen peas, pop out the pea between your finger and thumb. Discard the seed coat, as the fish usually ignore it.

Frozen foods

Frozen food is an excellent way of offering your fish foods that are close to their natural diet, but in a convenient form.

Right: This Fiji firefish (Nemateleotris decora) is a midwater feeder that easily captures food as it falls through the water. Here, it is about to capture a fragment of thawed-out shrimp.

Marine mix
This is a mixture of various natural marine invertebrate and fish meats.

Shrimp
Many wild-caught foods are irradiated to destroy disease pathogens.

Whole cockle
This natural food is accepted by all marine fish.

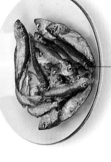

Fish
These small fish make excellent food for larger, "one-gulp" fish.

Krill
A nutritious food for larger fish; break up for small fish.

Immunity

As with people, fish have an array of natural defenses against infection. The most important of these is an intact skin – an obvious barrier to pathogen invasion. (The term "pathogen" means a disease-causing organism.)

Certain white blood cells roam the body, looking for pathogens that they then either "eat," or latch onto and destroy by discharging chemicals onto them.

Other white blood cells produce antibodies that stick to pathogens, helping the roaming white blood cells to recognize them for what they are and so destroy them.

The lining of the heart is important, as cells there capture and destroy bacteria found in the blood.

Skin and the mucus layer

A number of factors affect immunity. A mucus covering and an intact skin are an essential part of a fish's natural defense system. Incorrect handling, which strips off significant amounts of mucus, can be detrimental to the fish, and any damage that significantly cuts or abrades the skin will obviously increase the risk of infection.

The best way to avoid damaging fish when catching them is to use two soft nets, guiding the fish with one net into the second. The fish should then be transferred as quickly as possible. When dealing with large pond fish such as koi, the nets that reduce down to form an open-ended cylinder are very useful. As the koi is guided into the net, the narrow tube restricts its movement, preventing it from damaging itself. By taking hold of the narrow end of the tube of netting, you stop the fish from

escaping out of the other end during transfer. Always try to be calm and gentle while capturing fish. Chasing them to exhaustion will not only severely stress them, but can lead to a dangerously high buildup of lactic acid in their system, and may even kill some individuals.

Stress

Stress is an emotional and physical response to a problematic situation. Its function is to trigger an appropriate "reply" to that problem – one that best allows the fish to cope. This might involve flight, whereby the fish removes itself from the problem (say, a predator), or fight, where the fish attacks its problem and tries to drive it away (such as a territorial rival). Think of these behavioral responses as being initiated by the emotional part of stress. If a potential predator elicits a feeling of fear, then it is best to swim away from it as quickly as possible. The physical part is what the body does to facilitate these behaviors. It produces adrenaline, which quickens the heart rate to speed up blood flow to the muscles, and releases natural steroid hormones that trigger increased blood sugar production from energy stores in the body.

Stress itself becomes a problem when the cause of the stress is long-term and where fish cannot cope with the situation within their normal behavioral repertoire. The emotional aspect can be seen as altered behavior. For example, bullied fish will constantly

Excessive mucus production appears as a grayish film.

Clamped pectoral fin

Above: *Mucus is an important part of a fish's skin defense. Anything that irritates the skin, such as ectoparasites and water quality problems, will trigger an increase in the production of mucus.*

Below: *This rainbowfish is showing non-specific signs of illness, including clamped fins and loss of normal color pattern.*

fungal infections. Complex interactions with other hormones can lead to reproductive failure, because the sex organs do not develop properly.

Consider the example of naturally territorial fish such as convict cichlids (Archocentrus nigrofasciatus). In the wild they inhabit the rocky shores of Central American lakes, which are not very productive of food. Adequate space to find sufficient food for individuals or pairs and their young becomes an overriding necessity. These natural territories can be 2 m (6 ft) or so in diameter. Combined with these needs is the presence of large predatory fish, such as Parachromis dovii and the red devils (Amphilophus citrinellus and Amphilophus froebelii) that the convict cichlids must defend themselves and their fry against. It is therefore no surprise that convict cichlids are potentially very aggressive. If you group several convict cichlids into a 60-90 cm (24-36 in)-long aquarium, this will inevitably create a situation where one or two dominant individuals, or possibly

a mated pair, rule the whole aquarium as their territory and continually try to drive out the other cichlids. The less dominant fish become damaged by the aggressive attentions of the dominant pair, but because they cannot escape, they will try to hide out of fear (an emotional response). High levels of natural steroids progressively suppress the immune system, thereby increasing the risk of secondary infections in the already damaged skin and fins. The dominant individuals may suffer as well, living at a constantly high level of anxiety as they continually defend territory.

External factors such as low temperatures and poor water quality can all play a part in the suppression of a normal immune system.

Right: In the wild, this female convict cichlid would have to fight her own kind to establish a territory, and defend her young against other convict cichlids as well as larger predatory fish! In a crowded aquarium, these stressful activities can lead to ill health.

Above: A handling sock, which is a tube of netting, is an excellent way of controlling struggling fish as they are lifted from the water. Make sure the net is wet before you use it.

hide, while dominant fish may show heightened aggression to fish they cannot "get rid of." The physical side is more subtle. An unfortunate side effect of long-term production of natural steroids is immune suppression, as these hormones reduce the activity and production of new white blood cells. This means that stressed fish are more susceptible to infections. There is, for instance, a direct correlation between the blood level of steroids in fish and

Infectious diseases

The four main groups of infectious diseases are viral, bacterial, fungal, and parasitic. Parasitic diseases can be broadly divided into the microscopic single-celled protozoa, and the larger worms and crustaceans. Zoonoses are included here, but these are rare diseases that pose a minor risk to fishkeepers.

Viral diseases

Viruses are basically packages of genetic material that are visible only with the extreme magnification of an electron microscope. Viral diseases are probably more common than we realize, but their detection is difficult and relatively expensive. No direct treatments are available for viral infections in fish, so the best you can do is to support your fish by keeping them in the best possible conditions. Pay close attention to water quality, food, and the aquarium or pond environment to keep the fish's inbuilt immune systems at their best. Some commercial foods contain an immune stimulant, and these foods may be a useful way of enhancing your fish's natural defenses. There are a number of common viruses to be aware of.

Lymphocystis virus, a member of the *Iridovirus* family, triggers large, cauliflowerlike growths on the fins and skin of many species. Resist the urge to cut these off, as they will often disappear given time. An increased incidence of *Lymphocystis* has been associated with painted glassfish (*Chanda ranga*). In these fish, a colored dye is injected between the muscle masses to make the fish look highly colored, and this is probably how they become infected.

Carp pox is a herpes virus, and is seen on koi and goldfish during the colder months of the year. Just like cold sores in humans, this herpes virus appears when the fish is stressed, typically at times of low or rapidly fluctuating temperatures. It shows itself as white waxy growths on the fins and body, but these will usually disappear as the water temperature rises.

Spring viremia of carp is a rhabdovirus that causes hemorrhage, dropsylike signs (bloated body), and death. It affects mainly members of the carp family, such as koi and goldfish, but can infect other species, such as pike (*Esox lucius*) and the Wels catfish (*Silurus glanis*). If proven by laboratory tests, all

Above: This batfish (Platax teira) has a severe lymphocystis infection. The virus causes massive enlargement of individual cells, which appear as these obvious cauliflowerlike growths.

Below: The whitish candlewax-like lesions of carp pox are obvious on the fins and skin of this koi. As water temperatures rise they usually disappear, only to return again in the fall.

in-contact fish must be humanely destroyed. Alternatively, a movement order preventing any transfer of fish in or out of the premises is enforced for at least two years.

Bacterial diseases

Bacteria are huge in comparison to viruses. Present in large numbers in aquatic environments, they are often secondary invaders of cuts and abrasions, as well as causing diseases in their own right. Antibiotics are the most effective forms of treatments at present, although as with viruses, immune-enhancing foods and attention to husbandry will help. There are a number of important bacterial groups.

Pathogenic bacteria are well-recognized pathogens that have the ability to cause disease in their own right. One example is *Aeromonas salmonicida*, a bacterium that is able to attach to the healthy skin of fish and by producing toxic compounds, damage it and invade the deeper tissues. Originally described as affecting trout and salmon, varieties of this bacterium can cause real problems in ornamental koi and goldfish.

Opportunistic environmental bacteria are present in the surrounding environment and have the ability to cause serious disease if they get past the fish's immune system. Freshwater examples are *Aeromonas hydrophila, Pseudomonas, Flavobacterium,* and *Flexibacter columnaris*. In the marine aquarium, *Vibrio* species are the main potential pathogens. If any of these invade cuts, or lesions already made by other pathogens such as *Aeromonas salmonicida* or external parasites, they can multiply rapidly. Signs suggestive of bacterial infection are lethargy, loss of appetite, reddened areas (hemorrhages), ulceration, and abnormal swimming patterns.

Mycobacteria (also known as fish tuberculosis) are also, technically speaking, opportunist environmental bacteria, but they frequently affect fish in a different way than other types of bacteria. The course of the disease is often insidious, showing as a progressive loss of condition and wasting. Individual fish may be affected, but several may go down with the disease in the same aquarium or pond. The bacteria trigger inflammatory lesions called granulomas throughout the body, which disrupt normal organ function. If the liver is badly affected, the fish may die of liver disease; if the bones in the spine are infected, they may crumble, causing permanent deformity of the spine. Granulomas under the skin may erode onto the skin surface and appear as ulcers.

Below: This Trichogaster trichopterus is displaying signs typical of mycobacteriosis, or fish TB (tuberculosis). These include weight loss and skin ulceration.

Left: Damage to many different organs by a widespread bacterial infection can lead to ascites, or dropsy, a condition where fluid accumulates in the body cavity and scale pockets.

Left: Classic signs of septicemia in fish are hemorrhages – areas of bleeding on the skin and fins. Other signs include listlessness and loss of appetite.

Infectious diseases

How bacteria affect fish

Bacteria kill fish in three main ways. First, they can cause ulcers and skin hemorrhages that alter the permeability of the skin to water and salts, upsetting the fish's fluid and vital salt balance. This eventually affects the functioning of individual cells throughout all the organ systems, a situation that can lead to the death of the fish.

Some bacteria, such as *Flavobacterium*, release toxins that can damage the fish's brain and other nervous tissues, triggering abnormal swimming motions (known as shimmying) in susceptible fish such as mollies (*Poecilia sphenops*). Other toxins suppress the fish's immune system, removing its ability to "fight off" the bacteria.

Finally, bacteria can damage organ function. Extensive damage to vital organs such as the gills, kidneys, and liver will kill fish quite quickly.

Treatment for bacterial infections can be tricky. The best medicines are antibiotics, although these may not be easily available or easy to administer (see page 48). In addition to dealing with the infection, there may be secondary problems such as ulcers that may require packing to shore up this breach in the osmotic barrier, or keeping the fish in a mild salt solution to reduce osmotic imbalance.

Fungal disease

Fungal diseases can be a problem in both marine and freshwater fish. Some are very obvious, such as *Saprolegnia* infections, where characteristic white, cotton-wool-like patches are easy to see. Eventually, this kills the fish by creating an irreparable hole in

the fish's osmotic barrier, causing the same effects as bacterial ulcers. Others, such as *Ichthyophonus*, are much more difficult to diagnose, because the fungi are inside the fish, gradually damaging the internal organs until the fish dies. These are usually only diagnosed postmortem on laboratory examination.

Spores are present in most aquatic environments, but usually need some help before they can infect a fish. This comes in the form of cuts, abrasions, or bacterial ulcers. The mucus layer that covers the skin contains substances that inhibit the germination of fungal spores. If this is damaged or removed in some way, the spores can germinate to produce branching structures known as hyphae that invade dead and devitalized tissues to establish the infection.

Below: Ulcers caused by bacterial infections can be small, such as this one, or extensive, eroding deep into the underlying muscles and body cavity. Treatment can be difficult.

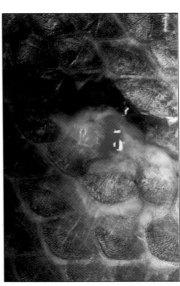

Fungi look like plants, but have similarities to animals in their physiology. This can make treatment difficult, as medications that are toxic to fungi are often toxic to fish. Treatments of choice include malachite green and phenoxyethanol. Povidoneiodine diluted to a 10% solution can be applied directly to the fungal lesion. Salt water will often inhibit the growth of freshwater *Saprolegnia*, even at a dilution down to 1-3 grams per liter.

Above: The tail of this cichlid has a growth of saprolegnia fungus toward the top, plus an area of (similar-looking) bacterial fin erosion at the lower righthand corner.

42

Protozoa, worms, and crustaceans

Protozoa are microscopic, single-celled animals. The most common ones are present on the outer surfaces of the skin and gills, although some can infect internal organs.

Ichthyophthirius multifiliis is the cause of the most familiar protozoan disease of freshwater fish, white spot. It is the free-swimming stages of this parasite that are the most susceptible to treatment. Higher temperatures speed up the life cycle, thereby exposing the susceptible stages sooner. In marine fish, Cryptocaryon irritans is also called white spot.

The disease usually presents itself by causing a loss of appetite, some skin irritation, and minor respiratory distress. Closer investigation will reveal pinhead-sized white to gray nodules. The parasite causes excessive irritation, resulting in exuberant mucus production and reactionary growth of the skin surface. This surface may eventually slough off, revealing large ulcers prone to secondary infection. The disease is highly infectious and often fatal within three to five days. The life cycle is complex and will continue in the aquarium until all the fish are dead or immune.

Chilodonella, Trichodina, and Tetrahymena are other protozoan parasites of freshwater fish. In large numbers, they are intensely irritant, stressing the fish and predisposing them to secondary infections.

Oodinium is the cause of velvet, or rust, disease. As these protozoa are parasitic for only part of their life cycle, numbers can build up in aquariums so that

Below: Cryptocaryon irritans is a common parasitic infestation of marine fish. It usually responds to copper-based treatments, but beware of their use in a tank containing invertebrates.

The white spots contrast starkly with darker areas of skin.

Left: This is a condition that is easy to diagnose – this mirror carp has white spot. The obvious white spots are areas where the parasites are attached, buried within the outer layers of the skin.

Protozoa, worms, and crustaceans

newly introduced fish can die within 12 hours. Infested fish show lethargy, loss of appetite, flicking, loss of normal coloration, and uncoordinated darting movements. Respiratory distress is common, as the gills are particularly vulnerable. Affected fish often have a yellowish, dusty appearance.

Amyloodinium (coral fish disease) is a rapidly progressing disease that starts off at the gills and shows initially as respiratory distress, but then spreads out across the skin. In addition to respiratory distress,

signs include skin rubbing and erratic swimming. Without treatment, death will occur within two days of respiratory symptoms.

Ichthyobodo (Costia) necatrix is considered a normal skin inhabitant that helps to remove sloughed tissue and mucus. If fish become immunosuppressed, the numbers of *Ichthyobodo* increase. Affected fish swim with fins clamped, but usually continue to feed.

Brooklynella and Uronema are similar in appearance, and seem to be of increasing importance. The infections are initially confined to the gills, but eventually spread, causing tissue irritation and skin loss that gives rise to ulcers. Fish become lethargic and secrete excess mucus. Death can occur within 12 hours of toxins being released by the protozoa.

Cryptosporidium nasoris is an internal protozoan that attaches to the lining of the gut of unicorn tangs (*Naso* spp.). Infected fish show emaciation, loss of appetite, and regurgitation, and produce droppings containing undigested food. Other protozoan parasites can invade the gallbladder, liver, kidneys, and even the gonads, effectively neutering the fish. Over 60 species of myxosporideal protozoa have been reported in marine fish.

Left: A discus with signs of head-and-lateral-line disease. The condition is often said to be associated with the protozoan parasite Hexamita, but the true cause may also involve environmental, bacterial, viral, and nutritional factors.

Externally parasitic protozoa are usually readily killed by proprietary ectoparasitic remedies ("ecto" meaning "outside"). These are widely available.

Flatworms

There are two groups of worm that are important: flatworms and roundworms. Flatworms include the ectoparasitic gill and skin flukes, and the endoparasitic tapeworms ("endo" meaning "inside"). The most common types encountered are gill flukes (*Dactylogyrus*) and skin flukes (*Gyrodactylus*). Both of these types are hermaphroditic (meaning they contain both male and female sexual organs).

Gill flukes are egglayers, mostly shedding their eggs into the water, where they hatch and the immature flukes seek out new hosts. The rate of reproduction of gill flukes is governed by the temperature of the water, so that at 1°C (34°F) the life cycle is five to six months, while this is reduced to only a few days at 24°C (75°F). Adult flukes feed on the cells of the gill tissue, blood, and the mucus produced in response to damage and irritation by the parasites.

Skin flukes give birth to live young. The difference is important, because the egg stage of the gill flukes is resistant to most medications, making repeat infestations common.

Other important flatworms that occasionally cause disease are tapeworms and the blood fluke *Sanguinicola inermis* – an occasional parasite of koi and other members of the carp family.

44

Roundworms

Roundworms are endoparasitic, and the most common of these is *Camallanus*, a worm that is often visible as an obvious cluster of worms sticking out of the fish's anus. This worm has two means of completing its life cycle. Eggs are shed into the general aquarium environment, where they develop into larvae that may be eaten, either by a fish or a crustacean. Once the larvae is eaten by a fish, it develops into a sexually mature adult. This is a *direct* life cycle.

If the egg is eaten by a crustacean – usually a copepod – the crustacean acts as an intermediate host, because the worm will develop part of the way to adulthood inside the crustacean before its host is eaten by a fish. It is only in the fish – the final host – that the worm's growth is completed. This is an *indirect* life cycle. The marine species all require intermediate hosts.

Treating worms can be difficult. Many of the brand name medicines against worms are relatively ineffective, and environmental concerns about the use of organophosphates have lead to a ban in the availability of these potentially toxic compounds in some countries.

Crustaceans

These distant relatives of crabs and shrimp are large parasites, visible to the naked eye. They are usually ectoparasites. Common crustacean parasites include *Argulus*, *Lernaea*, and *Ergasilus*.

Argulus, also known as the fish louse, is a large, disc-shaped parasite that is readily visible on its host. These parasites move quickly, shifting rapidly over the surface of the fish and can easily swim to new hosts. Irritant in themselves, they have been associated with triggering bacterial infections, introducing these pathogens accidentally with their mouthparts while feeding. They lay their eggs on plants and on the floor of ponds and aquariums, and can be resistant to medication.

Lernaea (anchor worms) do not look like crustaceans at all. They are static once attached, burying their heads and mouthparts into the fish's skin. Females look Y-shaped because they bear two egg sacs suspended from the tail end.

Ergasilus are highly modified crustaceans that latch onto and damage the gills.

All these parasites are hardy and resistant to most brand name fish medicines. The most effective ones contain the now heavily regulated organophosphate compounds. Where possible, these parasites are best removed individually.

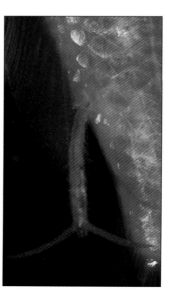

Above: The anchor worm buries its head into the skin of a fish, often allowing secondary invasion by bacteria. The two egg sacs at the back of the female give it a characteristic Y-shaped appearance.

Zoonoses and noninfectious diseases

Below: The reddened, raised areas on the skin are typical of the granulomas induced by fish mycobacteria when they invade cuts on the hand.

Zoonoses are diseases with the potential to be passed on from animals to people. Fortunately, the jump from fish to man is too great for the majority of diseases, so it is a rare problem in fishkeeping. Two notable exceptions are fish tuberculosis and Weil's disease.

Fish tuberculosis (fish TB) is caused by a group of bacteria called Mycobacteria, and manifests itself in people as raised inflamed lesions on the fingers and hands. Mycobacteria gain access beneath the skin by entering cuts, where they trigger a localized reaction called a granuloma. This condition rarely spreads further, as the bacteria cannot survive at higher core body temperatures. It usually responds well to antibiotics.

Weil's disease is caused by the bacterium *Leptospira icterohaemorrhagica* and is a zoonosis not from fish, but from wild rats. Pondkeepers are most at risk, as the bacteria can survive in water for a long time. Once again, this bacterium gains access through areas of damaged skin, but because it comes from a mammal it can live at higher temperatures. Although rare, it can cause serious liver and kidney damage. Avoid it by bandaging cuts, washing your hands with vinegar if you think you have been exposed, and deterring rats from around your pond.

Noninfectious diseases – tumors

Tumors, often referred to as cancers, can and do occur in fish, although they are often not diagnosed, and treatment at present is fairly rudimentary. In

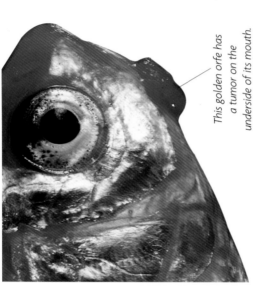

This golden orfe has a tumor on the underside of its mouth.

particular, older fish are more prone, and those fish that are regularly seen with tumors tend to be the longer-lived species, such as koi and goldfish. In goldfish in particular, red, well-defined raised masses on the skin are often seen. These typically are benign fibromas, or occasionally more malignant fibrosarcomas. Koi may develop skin tumors called erythrophoromas, which are derived from red pigment-bearing cells. In one case, skin tumors in koi have been tentatively linked to long-term exposure to poor water quality, a factor that may be significant in such long-lived fish.

A viral trigger for tumors has been described in swordtails (*Xiphophorus hellerii*) and platies (*Xiphophorus maculatus*). Internal tumors may

also occur. If they reach a large size they can produce an asymmetric appearance to the body, or cause balance disorders because of the compression or displacement of the swimbladder.

Nutritional deficiencies

Nutritional deficiencies, especially a lack of vitamin C, have been associated with spinal deformities in livebearers such as swordtails (*Xiphophorus hellerii*).

Electrocution

Fish in ponds subjected to lightning strikes have developed broken backs, probably due to massive contraction of the powerful back muscles during the electrical discharge.

Medications and treatments

If fish become diseased, it may be necessary to treat them. This is a procedure that should involve some thought; selecting random off-the-shelf medications is unlikely to be the best strategy.

Choosing a medication

Medicines available to fishkeepers fall into two main categories: brand name and restricted medicines.

Brand name medicines are the off-the-shelf products available from normal ornamental fish retail outlets. They are based on chemicals that have no restrictions on their use, and include mixtures of chemicals such as methylene blue, malachite green, formalin, and acriflavine. A word of caution, however. While many of these products are good (especially those formulated for treating ectoparasitic infestations), many antibacterial products are not so useful. This is because the testing of non-controlled medicines need not be so rigorous if they are to be used on ornamental fish rather than food fish. In some countries, such as the United States and in Asia, some antibiotics, such as oxytetracycline, come into this category as well. This widespread, unmonitored use has led to extensive oxytetracycline resistance in pathogenic bacterial populations. Also incorrect low dose rates of oxytetracycline can slightly suppress the immune system.

Depending on a country's drug laws, restricted medicines usually include the majority of antibiotics, many antiparasite medications (including organophosphates) and anesthetics. These products are usually available only from veterinarians, or pharmacists. There may be conditions attached to their provision.

Potential problems arise because very few of these drugs are marketed for or even tested on fish, or if they are, it is usually on fish of aquacultural importance, such as salmon or trout, and not on the huge array of ornamental species available. This

Calculating volumes

It is important to know the volume of a pond or aquarium when calculating how much medication to add to it. If you are unsure, here are some useful guidelines for calculating volumes.

Standard cuboidal aquariums and ponds:
Volume = length x width x depth.

Round, columnar aquariums:
Volume = depth x 3.142 x half the diameter².

Hexagonal aquariums:
The equation for round, columnar aquariums should be adequate, although the actual volume will be slightly less.

Ponds with varying depths:
Volume = average depth x length x width.
To calculate the average depth, add the greatest depth to the shallowest depth and divide by two.

Complex pond structures
"Divide" the pond into approximate shapes, calculate the volume for each shape, and add them all together to give a final volume.

Right: Calculating the volume of a natural-looking pond with a complex three-dimensional shape can be difficult. Estimating volume is usually adequate, as recommended medication dilutions are rarely extremely precise.

Medications and treatments

means that unforeseen drug reactions can be a risk. In addition, drug dose rates need to be estimated or extrapolated from known information, which can also give rise to toxicity problems or just result in a failure of the medicines to work!

Giving fish their medication

There are various methods of medicating fish, each with their own advantages and disadvantages.

In feed You can mix the medication with food and offer it to the fish. In theory, this is a good, non-stressful way of giving medicines, but there can be problems mixing drugs with fish food. Furthermore, sick fish are often off their food and if large numbers are present, some fish may not get enough medication, while others with larger appetites could take in too much. Before offering medicated food, starve the fish for 24 hours to make them hungry.

Bath Here, the fish is removed from its normal aquarium or pond and placed in a separate "bath" of medication. The disadvantage of this method is that the fish needs to be caught and handled, which is stressful. The good points are that dose rates can be calculated accurately for smaller containers, and there is no risk of creating unintentional effects on the filtration system.

In situ In this case, medication is added directly to the water in the pond or aquarium. Most brand name medications are used this way. It is nonstressful to the fish and easy for the fishkeeper

Preparing antibiotic-coated food

1 If the antibiotic is available only in pill form, carefully crush the required amount until it forms a fine powder. Always wear gloves while doing this.

2 Mix the powdered antibiotic with a small amount of vegetable oil until it forms a thick paste.

3 Combine this paste with an appropriate amount of pelleted food, coating it evenly. Allow the paste to air dry before feeding. Feed to 1% body weight, so if the fish weighs 100 gm (about 3.5 oz), feed it 1 gm (0.035 oz) of food per day. In practice, weights are difficult to judge. A 30 cm (12 in) koi will weigh about 500 gm (just over 1 lb), while an adult platy will weigh only 2-3 gm (1 oz). Use your best guess.

Adding medication to the aquarium

1 Calculate the correct amount of medication to be added to the tank, following the directions carefully. Fill a bottle or plastic container with water from the aquarium and add the medication to it.

to apply. A potential problem is that it may be difficult to estimate the volume of odd-shaped ponds or aquariums. (Many companies will give the volume of ponds and aquariums in literature supplied at the time of purchase – make a note of this and keep it in a safe place.) Even conventional shapes can pose problems if you try to allow for water displacement by gravel, ornaments, and so on. As a rule of thumb, for a well-furnished aquarium estimate a 10% volume displacement, so that if the volume of the bare aquarium is 100 liters (26 gallons), then its volume when fully furnished will be about 90 liters (24 gallons).

Another problem is that the biological filter may be at risk from certain medications, such as

antibiotics. Furthermore, the action of certain medications may be affected by water quality. Chloramine-T becomes more toxic in soft water, while the antibiotic oxytetracycline becomes less effective in hard water.

Using a hospital aquarium can eliminate many of these problems. Ideally, this is a dedicated aquarium of known volume that is set up along the same lines as a quarantine aquarium (and, indeed, a given aquarium or vat may double as both). Do not use activated charcoal in filters for hospital tanks, as this will remove many medications from the water.

Injections The advantage of injections is that you can ensure that the affected fish receives the correct dose of medication, but it does involve catching the fish, and larger fish may need sedating first. The used syringes and needles must be disposed of appropriately. Injecting is best left to fish health professionals, such as veterinarians.

Below: A spartan, dimly lit hospital tank is an ideal way of treating your sick fish away from the hubbub of the main aquarium.

3 Gently introduce the water containing the diluted medication back into the aquarium. Remember to keep any utensils solely for aquarium use.

2 Thoroughly mix the medication into the water. By diluting it first, you reduce the risk of producing localized spots of dangerously high concentrations.

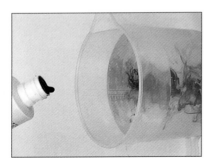

Medications and treatments

Quarantine

Quarantine can be a vital barrier against introducing infectious diseases into established collections. It involves keeping new fish in complete isolation from the main collection for a period of time. Freshwater and marine ornamental fish are kept in normal glass aquariums, while vats are commonly used for the larger pond fish. One advantage of quarantining is that it allows newly acquired fish time to adjust to new water conditions and husbandry regimes. Second, should the new fish be carrying any disease, this is liable to manifest itself during quarantine, giving you a chance to medicate and cure it before your main collection is put at risk.

Quarantine housing should be as simple as possible to allow accurate dosing of medication in an environment safely removed from your main fish or biological filtration.

For quarantine facilities to work properly, make sure that the water quality in the quarantine facility is as good as in your main display. If you do not do this, quarantined fish are likely to sicken while in quarantine, which is clearly an absurd situation!

A plastic plant will provide shelter for nervous fish in such a bare environment. An easily sterilizable plant pot also helps.

disease carriers and infect your quarantine facility. Only in marine aquariums, where the fish are more delicate, does this become a justifiable trade-off.

Instead, you will need to rely on physical and chemical methods of water purification. Zeolite in freshwater aquariums or vats will absorb ammonia excreted by the fish, and activated charcoal will adsorb many harmful chemicals from the water. A small protein skimmer in a marine aquarium would be of great benefit. More lavish setups could include ozonizers or ultraviolet sterilization.

Keep tank decorations to a minimum, providing just enough for nervous fish to hide behind. They should all be made of a material that is easy to clean, such as plastic. Avoid live plants and pieces of driftwood where possible, as these can act as disease reservoirs.

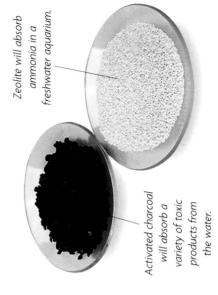

Zeolite will absorb ammonia in a freshwater aquarium.

Activated charcoal will absorb a variety of toxic products from the water.

Above: Aeration is important in vats and aquariums where normal filtration methods are absent. It enhances oxygen uptake and carbon dioxide loss at the water surface.

Equipping the quarantine tank

For quarantine to be successful, the water should be filtered, but in a quarantine tank you cannot rely on biological filtration. After each quarantine period the aquarium or vat will need to be dismantled and cleaned out with an iodine-based disinfectant. This means that you cannot use biological filtration, which takes time to establish. If you house some small fish in the aquarium to keep the biological filter "ticking over," there is a risk that they will act as

50

The quarantine period

Recommended quarantine periods can vary according to the diseases you are concerned about. However, a good guide would be a minimum of two weeks for all fish, extending to eight to twelve weeks for cold water fish at lower temperature ranges. (This is because most diseases will take longer to manifest at these temperatures.)

In general, it is not a good idea to medicate fish routinely, as many treatments can be stressful to the fish. The exception to this would be to treat all freshwater fish for white spot (*Ichthyophthirius*) and all marine fish for its saltwater equivalent *Cryptocaryon*, as these protozoal diseases are so common as to be almost ubiquitous. Better to deal with them here than in your main display tank.

Quarantine strategy

Temporarily house newly acquired fish in a quarantine tank.

After quarantine is completed, you can introduce the new fish into the existing community.

Remove sick fish to a separate hospital tank for treatment.

Each aquarium should have its own net and other equipment to prevent cross-contamination.

The tank is simply furnished, making it easy to treat, clean, or dismantle.

A display aquarium full of rockwork, gravel, plants, and your most prized fish.

A treatment tank is a clinical setup, designed for easy treatment and cleaning.

Euthanasia

If we are concerned about the welfare of our fish, then for some sick ones the only way to relieve their suffering is to dispose of them humanely. The ideal method should involve no stress prior to the act of euthanasia, and it should render the fish immediately insensible. Unfortunately, there are no perfect ways of doing this, but one method is to overdose the fish with a recognized fish anesthetic, such as MS222 or benzocaine. Alternatively, place the fish in a minimal amount of water and add as many Alka-Seltzer tablets as possible. The carbon dioxide released as the tablets fizz and dissolve will anesthetize and eventually kill the fish.

Another method is to deliver a quick, severe trauma to the back of the skull, using an angler's priest (a club or mallet for killing fish) or similar tool. This should at the very least stun the fish, and allows a follow-up humane decapitation to complete the procedure where necessary.

There are three disposal methods to be avoided at all costs. The first is death by hypothermia, usually by placing the fish in the freezer. This applies especially to temperate and cold water fish that are designed to endure low temperatures. Second, never flush a fish down the toilet. It may be out of sight and out of mind, but this method of disposal will not solve any welfare problems. Finally, never be tempted to do nothing. This extends the suffering of the fish unnecessarily and may leave it as prey to other fish that may kill it and scavenge on the corpse – an excellent way of passing on infectious diseases!

Some symptoms are obvious, such as finrot of the caudal fin on this Barbus everetti.

Diagnosis and treatment

Introduction

In this part of the book, we take a closer look at the more common problems seen within the main divisions of ornamental fishkeeping. Always consider water quality problems as a potential source of ill health in fish, especially when more than one fish is affected.

To help you arrive at a working diagnosis of the problem, the specific disease sections are tabulated by the main clinical signs (symptoms) and the species usually affected. Do bear in mind that these are not definitive diagnoses; an absolute identification of a disease problem would involve the microscopic examination of samples taken, or require laboratory techniques available to animal health professionals, such as veterinarians. In the absence of professional input of this kind, you are left with a "best guess" situation based on the behavioral signs and any visible abnormalities that the fish exhibit.

Suggested treatments are also included in the tables where appropriate. In the case of proprietary fish treatments, always follow the manufacturer's instructions and do not mix different medications without consulting the manufacturers first. For some other drugs, such as worming preparations, specific recommended dose rates are given, while for others, such as antibiotics, they are not. This is because a wide range of antibiotics is potentially available and recommended dose rates vary widely. Furthermore, some strains of bacteria are resistant to certain antibiotics, and it is impossible to predict which bacteria are resistant to which antibiotics. Ideally, a specific antibiotic should be used only after a sample of the bacterium has been cultured in the laboratory and exposed to a range of different antibiotics to assess its spectrum of resistance – a process often referred to as "culture and sensitivity" testing.

Organophosphates are also mentioned, as these are readily available in many countries. However, in some areas of the world their use is restricted. Because of these variations in availability, dose rates will need to be ascertained from the manufacturers or from the fish health professionals supplying the product.

SPECIFIC PROBLEMS – Tropical freshwater fish

The keeping of tropical freshwater aquariums covers a wider spectrum of fish species – and therefore husbandry requirements – than those encountered in marine or cold water fishkeeping. The two extremes of soft, acidic discus aquariums and hard, alkaline Rift Valley lake aquariums have already been mentioned. In addition to varying water quality needs, the differing natural habitats from which these fish have evolved means that aquarium setups can vary quite widely. They can range from mimicking the warm, still drainage ditches of Southeast Asia enjoyed by members of the fighting fish family (*Betta* species), to the fearsome rapids of Africa inhabited by the cichlid *Teleogramma brichardi*. This variety of needs, and whether we are

meeting them, must be considered when evaluating the health, or illness, of freshwater fish.

Most of the species offered for sale are captive-bred, but those from Asia or the southern United States are often pond-reared, which can mean that fish may still carry "wild-type" infections, such as tapeworms and gill flukes. In addition, many live-bearers, such as guppies and mollies, are reared in salt water and are acclimatized to fresh water only prior to export. This may help to explain the susceptibility of this group of fish to common freshwater pathogens in the home aquarium. Countries not usually considered as hotbeds of ornamental fish production, such as Czechoslovakia, are becoming more important as producers of quality aquarium-bred and reared fish.

Above: This dwarf cichlid is displaying signs consistent with shock – dark colors but raised fins. The fishkeeper's task is to establish the cause and take the appropriate remedial action.

Behavioral abnormalities

Main sign	Other signs	Species affected	Possible diagnoses	Treatments
Loss of balance	Rapid breathing	All	Ammonia or nitrite poisoning	Address water quality problem
	Pale gills, ulcers, death	Deep angelfish (*Pterophyllum altum*)	Deep angelfish disease (a virus)	None
	Dark coloring, disorientation, and whirling; sudden death	All	Bacterial meningitis	Antibiotics

Abnormal behavior is often the first sign of disease. The white spots of Ichthyophthirius are just visible on these Pimelodus catfish.

Loss of balance	Lethargy, pale skin, protruding eyes, sex reversal in guppies (female to male)	All	*Ichthyophonus* (internal fungal infection)	None
Scratching (flashing)	Graying of skin (excessive mucus production), reddened areas of skin, rapid respiration	All	Ectoparasitic infestation (protozoan or skin fluke)	Brand name ectoparasite remedy. If skin flukes, consider praziquantel at 10 mg/liter for a three-hour bath.
Respiratory distress. One-sided breathing in discus.	Clamped fins, flashing	All	Gill flukes	Brand name ectoparasite preparations. Also praziquantel at 10 mg/liter, three-hour bath.
Aimless swimming (shimmying)	Loss of balance, death	All, but live-bearers especially affected	Flavobacterium infection	Antibiotics
Headstanding	Dark brown gills	Tiger barbs	Nitrite poisoning	Address water quality problem. For high nitrite levels in freshwater systems add 1-3 gm/liter salt indefinitely.
Lethargy	Loss of appetite, lack of coordination, emaciation, death	Ramirez dwarf cichlid (*Microgeophagus ramirezi*)	Ramirez dwarf cichlid virus	None
	Death	Texas cichlid (*Herichthys cyanoguttatum*), convict cichlid (*Archocentrus nigrofasciatus*), *Tilapia zillii.*	Rio Grande perch rhabdovirus	None
	Reddened areas of skin, feeding stops	All	Bacterial septicemia	Antibiotics

TROPICAL FRESHWATER FISH – Physical abnormalities

Main sign	Other signs	Species affected	Possible diagnoses	Treatments
Weight loss	Listlessness	All, but especially wild-caught Malawi cichlids	*Acanthocephalus* worms	Worming. Levamisol at 2 mg/liter for up to 24 hours. Benzimidazoles such as fenbendazole at 20 mg/kg body weight given seven days apart, or mebendazole at 20 mg/kg for three treatments given at weekly intervals.
	Diarrhea, darkened coloration	Discus	Capillaria worms	Worming. Levamisol at 2 mg/liter for up to 24 hours. Benzimidazoles such as fenbendazole at 20 mg/kg body weight given seven days apart, or mebendazole at 20 mg/kg for three treatments given at weekly intervals.
	Poor growth	All	Tapeworms	Worming with praziquantel, and avoid feeding live foods.
	Weakness	Orange and green chromides (*Etroplus maculatus* and *E. suratensis*)	Chromide iridovirus	None
	Feeding stops, regurgitation of food, diarrhea, death	Angelfish (*Pterophyllum* species)	*Cryptosporidium* (an internal protozoan)	Difficult. Try sulphonamide antibiotics, but success unlikely.

The hollow belly of this goodeid live-bearer is an obvious sign of weight loss.

Weight loss				
	Darkened color, excessive mucus production, rapid respiration, lethargy	Discus. Occasionally angelfish (*Pterophyllum* species).	Discus plague. Unknown cause	None
	Emaciation	All	Coccidia (internal protozoa)	May respond to anticoccidial drugs, such as amprolium, as a continuous bath at 10 mg/liter for 7-10 days or to sulphonamide antibiotics.
	Spinal curvature, open skin sores, protruding eyes	All	Fish tuberculosis (TB)	Difficult. Potential zoonosis, so consider euthanasia.
	Muscle wastage	All, especially large, fast-growing fish fed on dead fish	Vitamin E deficiency	Correct diet

Below: The most common cause of a bent spine in ornamental fish is considered to be fish tuberculosis. Other possibilities include nutritional deficiencies and electrocution.

S-shaped curvature of the spine.

Right: Changes in coloration can be important clues to disease. Darkening in discus is non-specific, but it does definitely indicate a sick discus!

57

TROPICAL FRESHWATER FISH – Physical abnormalities

Main sign	Other signs	Species affected	Possible diagnoses	Treatments
Obvious red worms protruding from anus	Weight loss, ulceration around anus	All, especially live-bearers	*Camallanus* worms	Worming. Levamisol at 2 mg/liter for up to 24 hours. Benzimidazoles such as fenbendazole at 20 mg/kg body weight given seven days apart, or mebendazole at 20 mg/kg for three treatments given at weekly intervals.
Enhanced coloration	Wasting	All, especially Malawi cichlids	Hemoparasites (protozoa in the blood)	Methylene blue at 100 mg/liter for a 24-hour bath, or metronidazole at 50 mg/liter. Refresh every day.
Swollen abdomen	Raised scales, protruding eyes	All	Dropsy, multiorgan failure, usually due to bacterial infection.	Antibiotics. Outlook poor.
		Malawi cichlids	Malawi bloat (unknown cause – viral, bacterial, and protozoal causes suggested)	Optimize water conditions. Possibly use antibiotics.
Obvious body symmetry abnormalities	Lumps and growths, deep ulcerative sores, loss of appetite, wasting.	All, especially older fish	Tumors	Smaller tumors on the skin and fins may be suitable for surgery, otherwise outlook poor.
Spinal curvature	Open skin sores, wasting, and protruding eyes	All fish	Fish tuberculosis (TB)	See above

Spinal curvature	Poor growth	Especially live-bearers	Vitamin C deficiency	Correct diet. Offer more greens/algae.
Ulceration	Reddened fins and skin, frayed fins, feeding stops, listlessness	All	Bacterial infection	Antibiotics
	Whitish erosive areas, especially along back of fish, mouth fungus, and shimmying	Mollies (mouth fungus and shimmying); guppies (tail rot), neon tetra (false neon tetra disease).	Flexibacter columnaris (bacterial infection)	Antibiotics
	Blindness	All	Fusarium (fungal infection)	Difficult
		Snakeheads	Striped snakehead skin ulcerative disease (viral infection)	None
Ulcers in the head and along the lateral line.	Slimy droppings, weight loss, no appetite, secondary infections	Discus, angelfish, oscars, and other cichlids	Hole-in-the-head disease, multifactorial. May be protozoal, bacterial, dietary, poor environment, or viral.	Improve water conditions. Try metronidazole or other antibiotic.

Painful erosive lesions around the mouth may stop the fish from feeding.

Marked swelling of the eye has displaced it from the socket.

Right: Tumors can occur in any fish as a result of age, genetic, or environmental factors. This Heterandria formosa has a tumor in the vent region.

Right: Pop-eye (or exophthalmia), as seen in this speckled molly, can be due to one of several possibilities, from a tumor behind the eye to a bacterial infection. Alternatively, it may be part of a more generalized problem, such as dropsy.

59

TROPICAL FRESHWATER FISH – *Physical abnormalities*

Main sign	Other signs	Species affected	Possible diagnoses	Treatments
Black spots		Wild-caught fish, especially silvery/light colored fish	Trematodes (flatworms)	Rarely cause problems. Consider praziquantel.
Graying skin (excessive mucus production)	Clamped fins, depression, sudden death	All	Chilodonella (protozoan ectoparasite)	Ectoparasitic preparations
	Skin ulcers, breathing problems	All	Trichodina (protozoan parasite)	Brand name ectoparasitic medication
	Reddening of skin, ulceration	All	Skin flukes (flatworms)	Ectoparasitic preparations
White tufts on surface	Ulceration	All	Epistylis (Heteropolaria) (protozoan parasite)	Ectoparasitic preparations
	Ulceration, secondary bacterial infections	All	Saprolegnia (fungal disease)	Brand name fungal medication
Obvious discrete white spots	Breathing difficulties, irritation, fins clamped	All	White spot (protozoan parasite)	Brand name white spot remedy
Whitish areas or "spots"	Ulceration; often associated with bacterial infections and white spot	Live-bearers, cichlids (especially dwarf cichlids) and tetras.	Tetrahymena (protozoan parasite)	Try brand name ectoparasitic medication. Can spread internally, so treatment may not work.
Large, cauliflowerlike masses on fins and skin		All	Lymphocystis (viral infection)	None – usually self-limiting
Obvious nodules	Dark or accentuated coloring, weight loss, whirling, and finrot	All	Sporozoa (protozoan parasites)	No treatment

Symptom	Sign	Fish affected	Cause	Treatment
Dusty effect over body surface	Breathing difficulties	All	Velvet disease (protozoan parasite)	Brand name velvet treatment. Metronidazole at 50 mg/liter for up to 24 hours daily for 10 days, or quinine hydrochloride at 10-20 mg/liter indefinitely. Some fish sensitive.
Whitened areas of muscle	Loss of color, emaciation, spinal curvature	Neon tetras, other small tetras, killifish	Neon tetra disease (protozoan parasite)	None
Pale patches	Stringy, white feces	Discus, kissing gouramis	*Protopalina* (protozoan parasite)	Brand name ectoparasitic medication
Obvious large, parasite	Irritation, ulceration	All	Fish louse (*Argulus*) or *Livoneca*	Remove parasites individually or treat with organophosphates.
	Flatworms on glass and substrate		Planaria	Not parasitic. May indicate overfeeding.
Damage to skin and/or loss of eyes and fins	Secondary bacterial infections	All	Trauma	Antibiotics. Alter and improve management.

Left: *Lymphocystis is the viral disease that is most easily recognized because it causes the obvious, whitish swellings typical of the infection. The affected fish here is a Chanda ranga.*

Left: *The ulcer on this male Labidochromis caeruleus will certainly have a bacterial infection, but was it due to a bite, a parasitic infestation, or a genuinely nasty strain of bacteria?*

SPECIFIC PROBLEMS – Cold water and pond fish

From the point of view of disease, cold water aquarium and pond fish can be grouped together, because in most cases the same species of fish are kept in both environments. The main difference in their health management is that in temperate countries, such as the northern United States, the UK, and most of the rest of Europe, pond fish are subjected to seasonal temperature variations. This has a number of important effects on their well-being.

Seasonal diets

During the late fall, as average water temperatures fall, fish are less able to digest their food properly. This applies especially to protein digestibility, so it is better to feed a lower protein food at this time of year. Reduced digestibility can also lead to a bacterial overgrowth on undigested protein left in the gut. Many pond owners will switch to a wheat germ-based food at this time. At temperatures below 8-10°C (46-50°F), the general advice is not to offer food, as most fish (barring true cold water fish such as trout) will not take it. Most mature ponds will provide "light snacks" in the form of invertebrates or plant material that the fish can scavenge if they are slightly hungry, without the risk of overfeeding them. These processes are reversed in the spring, as water temperatures rise.

The immune system

As the water cools, the fish's immune system becomes suppressed, so that they are less able to deal with infections. (Fortunately, most disease processes are also slowed down at lower temperatures). This is when you may see the first signs of carp pox on koi or a recurrence of bacterial septicemias and ulcers. These should be attended to immediately. If possible, it is worthwhile gently catching each and every fish in early fall and giving them a quick examination to check for small ulcers, external parasites, etc. Treat any obvious lesions or infections.

There are other seasonal considerations that will help to ensure the healthy survival of your fish, such as maintaining the pond filter system and keeping the water clear of decaying vegetation. Here, we look at each of these aspects in more detail.

Filters

Filters should be cleaned out in the fall. Pond fish spend the coldest months of the year in a state of apparent dormancy, surviving off energy stores of

Above: During winter, movement of the water surface will help to prevent ice formation, but too great a volume turnover can be harmful.

abdominal fat. They live in a deeper, static layer of water, but due to the unusual properties of water, this will remain at about 4°C (39°F). Therefore, if you have the facility, you should change the pond intake from a bottom drain to one partway up the water column. This tends to preserve the static layer, regardless of the weather above the surface. In ponds without this facility, or that are not deep enough, the fish are subjected to a constant water flow, forcing them to swim and use up valuable energy reserves. Reducing the water flow will help, but do not stop it altogether, as the bacterial colonies, necessary for the filter to function, will be starved of oxygen.

Above: Appetite and food digestion in temperate fish such as these fancy goldfish is strongly correlated with temperature.

Clearing the pond

Vegetation in the water comes from in and around the pond, and if left to decompose, water quality can suffer. Fall is the time to cut back water lilies and other plants as their leaves start to die. Leaves from surrounding deciduous trees are best dealt with by covering the pond with a net or using a skimmer.

Dormancy

During the winter, pond fish appear to enter a state of hibernation. This is not a true hibernation, as they can still respond to stimuli, although their sluggish responses may be due to their inability to react at these low temperatures, rather than a reduced perception of a stimulus. Breaking any ice that forms at the surface with a hammer is not a good idea, as it will send shock waves through the water. These will be sensed by the fish's lateral line – a shock that may be too much in their vulnerable state. A floating heater will keep an area of the surface clear, allowing carbon dioxide to escape from solution in the water and also enabling some oxygen to dissolve into it.

Behavioral abnormalities

Main sign	Other signs	Species affected	Possible diagnoses	Treatments
Sudden death, especially in ponds	Sudden onset of spinal deformities	All	Electrocution/lightning strike	No treatment
Respiratory distress	Gray spots on gills and fins	All – usually pond fish	Glocchidia (larval mussels)	Usually self-limiting
Scratching and irritation	Gray skin due to excessive mucus production, reddened skin, ulceration	All	Skin flukes	Proprietary ectoparasitic preparations. Praziquantel at 10 mg/kg by mouth.
Weakness	Wasting and anemia	All	Hemoparasites (protozoa found in the blood)	Methylene blue at 100 mg/liter for a 24-hour bath, or metronidazole at 50 mg/liter. Refresh every day.
Lethargy	Loss of appetite, hemorrhages	Golden shiner (Notemigonus crysoleucas)	Golden shiner virus	No cure
Loss of balance, unable to swim down from surface or up from bottom		All, but especially fancy goldfish	Swimbladder dysfunction	Usually no treatment for fancy goldfish. Try antibiotics if you suspect bacterial infection.
Sudden darting movements	Loss of balance, rapid respiration	All	Sudden onset of water poisoning, new tank syndrome	Address water quality problem

63

COLD WATER AND POND FISH – Physical abnormalities

Main sign	Other signs	Species affected	Possible diagnoses	Treatments
Ulceration	Reddened fin and skin, frayed fins, feeding stops; listlessness	All	Bacterial infection	Antibiotics
	Blindness	All	Fusarium (fungal infection)	Difficult
Graying skin (excessive mucus production)	Clamped fins, depression, sudden death	All	Chilodonella (protozoan ectoparasite)	Ectoparasitic preparations
	Skin ulcers, breathing problems	All	Trichodina (protozoan parasite)	Brand name ectoparasitic medication
	Reddening of skin, ulceration	All	Skin flukes (flatworms)	Ectoparasitic preparations
White tufts on surface	Ulceration	All	Epistylis (Heteropolaria) – protozoan parasite	Ectoparasitic preparations
	Ulceration, secondary bacterial infections	All	Saprolegnia (fungal disease)	Brand name fungal medication
Obvious discrete white spots	Breathing difficulties, irritation, fins clamped	All	White spot (protozoan parasite)	Brand name white spot remedy
Large, cauliflowerlike masses on fins and skin		All	Lymphocystis (viral infection)	None – usually self-limiting
Obvious nodules	Dark or accentuated coloring, weight loss, whirling, and finrot	All	Sporozoa (protozoan parasites)	No treatment

A stickleback with a sporozoan infestation.

Symptoms		Affected fish	Disease	Treatment
Dusty effect over body surface	Breathing difficulties	All	Velvet disease (Oodinium) – protozoan parasite	Proprietary velvet treatment. Metronidazole at 50 mg/liter for up to 24 hours daily for 10 days, or quinine hydrochloride at 10-20 mg/liter indefinitely. Some fish sensitive.
Obvious large, disc-shaped parasites	Irritation, ulceration	All	Fish louse (Argulus)	Remove parasites individually or treat with organophosphates.
Obvious Y-shaped parasites	Ulceration, irritation	All	Anchor worm (Lernaea)	Remove parasites individually, or treat with organophosphates.
Candlewax-like masses on skin and fins	Retarded growth	Cyprinids, especially carp/koi	Carp pox	No treatment. Will usually clear up in warmer water.
Weight loss	"Big head" in carp, swollen abdomen	All	Tapeworms	Praziquantel at 10 mg/kg body weight in food
Long trails of feces	Loss of balance	All, especially fancy goldfish	Constipation/diarrhea	Feed higher fiber foods
Cysts in skin and muscles		Koi	Dermocystidium (fungal disease)	Surgical removal
Opacity of lens in eye		All, especially pond fish	Diplostomum (intermediate stage of bird tapeworm)	No cure. Control snails as source of disease.
Emaciation	Sunken eyes, diarrhea	Carp and koi	Eimeria (gut protozoa)	May respond to anticoccidial drugs, such as amprolium (as a continuous bath at 10 mg/liter for 7-10 days) or to sulphonamide antibiotics.
Swollen abdomen	Scales not protruding, loss of balance	Goldfish	Hoferrellus carassii (protozoan parasite)	No effective treatment

COLD WATER AND POND FISH – *Physical abnormalities*

Main sign	Other signs	Species affected	Possible diagnoses	Treatments
Scales protruding, hemorrhages		All	Dropsy (also known as ascites), often secondary to heart, gill, and kidney disease.	Try antibiotics. Poor outlook.
	Large, wormlike parasite	Pond fish	Leeches	Remove parasites individually, or treat with organophosphates.
Protruding eyes	Hemorrhages	Grass carp	Grass carp rheovirus	No cure
Whitish tufts on hood		Hooded fancy goldfish	Mucus "tufts"	Normal. No treatment needed.
Open skin sores, wasting, and protruding eyes	Spinal curvature	All	Fish tuberculosis	Consider euthanasia, especially because of the risk of spreading to humans.
Ulceration, loss of balance	Nonsymmetrical swelling	All	Tumors	Surgery or euthanasia
Raised white nodules on gill covers and leading edges of pectoral fins. Nodules may be very swollen.		Goldfish and other cyprinids	Nuptial tubercles of males	Normal in reproductively active males
Hemorrhages, mucoid fecal casts, lethargy	Swollen abdomen	Carp, koi, goldfish; occasionally pike and Wels catfish	Spring viremia of carp virus	No cure
Inflamed areas, hemorrhages	Damage to skin and/or loss of eyes and fins	All	Trauma, with secondary bacterial infection	Antibiotics. Alter and improve management.
	Wasting	Carp and koi	Vitamin E deficiency (Sekoke disease)	Vitamin E supplement. Change diet.

Symptoms	Disease	Fish	Treatment
Mottled colored gills, weak, lethargic	Branchiomycosis (fungal)	Cyprinids	No known cure
Damaged gills	Gill necrosis virus	Cyprinids	No cure
Extensive gill damage and hemorrhage	Sanguinicola inermis (parasitic fluke)	Cyprinids	Praziquantel at 10 mg/kg body weight in food. Control snails (intermediate hosts).
Damaged gills, obvious large parasites	Ergasilus (gill maggot)	Cyprinids	Remove parasites individually, or treat with organophosphates.
Excess mucus production, clamped fins, depression, sudden death	Chilodonella (protozoa)	All	Brand name ectoparasitic medications or glacial (concentrated) acetic acid dips at 2 ml/liter for 30-45 seconds. May kill weak fish.
Clamped fins, scratching, and flashing. Inactivity.	Gill flukes	All	Brand name ectoparasitic preparations. Also praziquantel at 10 mg/liter – three-hour bath.
Excess mucus production, irritation, mass deaths	Ichthyobodo (Costia) necatrix (protozoan parasite)	All	Usual ectoparasitic treatments
Thickened gills, mucus trailing from gills	Environmental gill disease	All	Correct environmental problem. Try chloramine-T at 10 mg/liter. Use less in soft water, down to 2 mg/liter.

Respiratory distress

Huge numbers of gill flukes can cause extensive damage to the delicate gills.

Right: Extreme systemic disease affecting many organs can cause a huge accumulation of fluids inside the body cavity and beneath the scales. Correctly called ascites, this condition is very often known to aquarists as dropsy.

Right: Leeches not only cause irritation and damage to the skin, but they can also transmit infections. They are usually encountered in natural ponds.

Keeping tropical marine fish and invertebrates

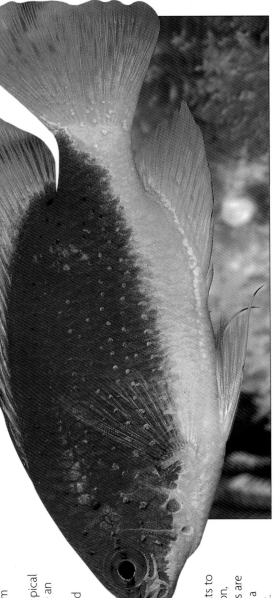

The successful management of a marine aquarium requires an extra set of skills and knowledge in addition to those needed to keep freshwater tropical fish. It is important to remember that oceans are an extremely stable environment, so aside from boundary zones, such as rockpools, estuaries, and mangrove swamps, daily and even seasonal variations in water quality and temperature are narrow. This means that many marine organisms appear to have only a limited ability to respond and adapt to major alterations in their environment because there has been no evolutionary pressure on them to do otherwise. Therefore, when these creatures are transferred from their native habitats to aquariums, everything must be perfect. In addition, the vast majority of marine fish and invertebrates are wild-caught. This means that they all arrive with a certain number of parasites, bacteria, viruses, etc.

Here are a few important points to bear in mind when keeping marine tropical fish.

Behavior

Many reef fish, such as damsels and angelfish, are territorial, vigorously defending either an individual or a pair's territory against all other fish, especially members of the same species. This behavior, essential on a highly populated reef, may cause problems in the confines of a small aquarium.

An alternative lifestyle is that of shoaling fish, which congregate in large schools. This not only reduces an individual's chances of being eaten, but also helps to maximize the use of certain food

Above: Chrysiptera taupou is a damselfish that, like most of its related species, is so territorial that its behavior can cause serious consequences in the home aquarium.

resources and to increase the opportunities for spawning. Pseudanthias spp. are classic examples of shoaling fish. However, due to the low stocking densities of marine aquariums, the relatively high price of individual fish and the tendency of many aquarists to keep "one of each," these fish are rarely kept in the correct social numbers or groupings. This not only stresses the fish, but also deprives the

aquarist of the chance of achieving the ultimate pinnacle – successfully breeding marine fish.

Water quality

Probably more so than for other branches of fishkeeping, good water quality management is the cornerstone of marine fishkeeping.

Oxygen Seawater holds less oxygen than freshwater, so there is an increased risk of overstocking marine fish. Excessively high temperatures will reduce the oxygen-holding capacity of the water and stress the fish. (See page 17 for recommended temperatures.)

Redox potential This is a complex concept, but think of it as a measurement of a body of water's ability to support life. Water with a high redox potential is of high quality, with plenty of surplus oxygen. Low redox potential waters have low oxygen levels due to excessive waste materials, including large amounts of organic waste from overstocking or debris.

Redox is measured on the p scale of 0 to 42, with 0 as the lowest quality and 42 the highest quality. Normal values range from about 27 to 32.

pH levels

The pH of seawater is usually high, about 8.3. At this level, more ammonia is in the toxic, nonionized form (see page 18). Bear this in mind should you correct a drop in pH, because as you raise the pH, a significant amount of ammonia present will convert to the toxic, nonionized form.

Seawater has a significant intrinsic buffering capacity that is backed up by other calcium or magnesium carbonate-containing aquarium furniture, such as coral sand or dolomite. However, carbon dioxide and other metabolic by-products from the aquarium inhabitants will tend to reduce the pH. This will be resisted to some extent by the normal buffering already described, but can be exhausted, leading to a rapid fall in pH.

High levels of phosphates complicate this further, by forming layers of a mineral coating of calcium phosphate, calcium fluoride, and calcium chloride over substances containing magnesium and calcium carbonate, such as dolomite. The substances are then no longer able to react with the water, so their buffering ability is gone. In tanks with a heavy algal growth, the opposite may occur during the period of illumination and all the available carbon dioxide is removed from the water.

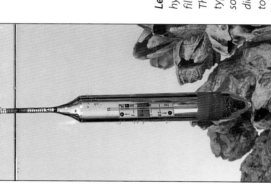

Left: The classic hydrometer is an air-filled, glass float. There are other types available, some of which have a dial-like arrangement to help you read the specific gravity.

Salinity

Salinity is a measure of the salt content of water. Correctly it is measured as milligrams of sodium chloride (salt) per deciliter. This is usually abbreviated to mg/dl, or more commonly ppt (parts per thousand). True seawater has a salinity of about 34-37 ppt. The amount of salt dissolved in a sample of water affects its density, so in practice, the salt content is estimated by measuring its density, or specific gravity (S.G.), using a hydrometer.

A hydrometer is usually an air-filled glass float with a top section that rises above the water surface. A scale is included in this top section. The specific gravity is read off the scale at the level of the water surface. Pure water has a S.G. of 1.000. The more salt there is dissolved in the water, the denser it becomes and so the hydrometer is displaced upward, altering the reading. Most marine aquariums are kept at an S.G. of 1.020 to 1.023. The Red Sea is very salty, with a S.G. of 1.025 and over! Water density is affected by temperature, so you may see the specific gravity stated for a particular temperature.

The water surrounding a marine fish is more concentrated than the body fluids of the fish, so osmosis constantly draws water from the fish. To prevent dehydration, saltwater fish must drink and the salt they imbibe is excreted via the mucus-secreting glands of the skin, in the feces, but primarily from the kidneys and the gills. Sudden alterations in the salinity of the water will dramatically upset this delicate balance, stressing or even killing the animal. Salinity also affects dissolved oxygen levels; higher salinity reduces oxygen levels, which is why many marine aquarists keep the S.G. at the lower ranges of 1.020 to 1.022.

Environmental toxins

Environmental toxins include ammonia, nitrite, heavy metals, chlorine, chloramine, and nicotine (cigarette smoke), all of which can have a detrimental effect on water quality. Of the heavy metals, copper is probably the most important, because it is toxic to invertebrates at low concentrations and to fish at higher concentrations. However, it is an important constituent of many off-the-shelf medications. Copper can bind to rockwork in the aquarium, only to be slowly released at a later date, a fact that can result in invertebrate losses some time after medications containing copper were last used. Fortunately, copper test kits are readily available.

Marine fishkeepers will also come across some concepts and equipment not normally used with freshwater aquariums.

Keeping tropical marine fish and invertebrates

Protein skimmers

Protein skimming makes use of the fact that organic molecules accumulate at an air-water interface. Forcing vast numbers of tiny bubbles from an airstone up through a water column allows all these organic molecules to accumulate at the water surface, where they form a stable foam. This foam can be collected and removed from the aquarium.

The advantage of this system is that it dramatically reduces the waste load on the biological filters. However, it can also remove beneficial organic compounds, such as dissolved vitamins, so for this reason some aquarists will run the protein skimmer for only half the day.

The stable foam will form only in water containing salt, so although it cannot be used in freshwater aquariums, it can be used in systems with very low salt levels, such as brackish water ones, where it will work with salt levels as low as 5 ppt.

How a protein skimmer works

Protein-laden foam overflows into this cup and settles out into a discardable liquid.

Air bubbles rising up the central tube attract protein from the water. The foam progresses upward, while the cleaned water continues its longer path toward the outlet.

Cleaned water returns to the aquarium from the outer cylinder of the skimmer.

Air drawn into the venturi creates a mass of bubbles in the water flow.

Water intake from the aquarium.

Ozone

Under the influence of an electric charge, oxygen molecules can take on an extra oxygen atom so that instead of being O_2, they become O_3. These new oxygen molecules are unstable and are known as ozone. In nature, this happens following a lightning strike, when you can smell the characteristic fresh smell of ozone in the air. Because of this instability, the O_3 molecules easily give up the third oxygen atom with a release of energy when they meet another substance. This

oxidizing reaction can be considered a form of chemical burn. Marine fishkeepers can create ozone in a device called an ozonizer; air is blown across a minute electrical discharge to create the ozone, which is then bubbled into the aquarium. Any bacteria or free-swimming parasites that come into contact with the ozone are burned and destroyed by the release of stored energy. Normally, the fish are protected from the damaging effects of ozone because it is bubbled up through a protective uplift tube or incorporated into the airflow into a protein skimmer. Ozone can be used in freshwater as well.

Ultraviolet (UV) sterilization

White light is formed from a continuum of colors called the spectrum. Some of the light in that part of the spectrum known as ultraviolet is damaging to tissues. (In people, sunburn is the result of the action of ultraviolet light from the sun on skin). Ultraviolet sterilization involves pumping aquarium water past fluorescent tubes emitting ultraviolet light, so that any pathogens exposed to this light are damaged.

Remember that the efficacy of ultraviolet sterilization depends on a number of factors. The first is the length of time that the pathogens are exposed to the ultraviolet light, which in turn depends on the length of the tube and the flow rate past it. Second, ultraviolet light does not penetrate water very deeply, so a narrow column of water is needed to allow maximum penetration. Third, any algae, bacteria, or debris that stick to the side of the tube will reduce the amount of light penetrating the water. Finally, the ultraviolet output from the fluorescent tubes reduces over time, so change the tubes at intervals according to the manufacturer's instructions, usually every six months. The tubes are also expensive, because they must be made of quartz glass, as ordinary glass filters out UV light.

Ultraviolet units are also frequently used in ponds to reduce suspended algae. Installed in the pipeline to the water inlet to filters, they work by damaging any free-floating algae. This causes them to clump together to allow easy retention by the filter media. These units are unlikely to be of sufficient capacity to act as true sterilizers for large bodies of water.

Lighting

This is not usually an issue with fish, although anecdotally, bright lights have been associated with blindness in nocturnal fish such as lionfish (*Pterois* species). However, it does become important with many marine invertebrates. Many of the commonly kept reef invertebrates, including anemones, hard and soft corals, and *Tridacna* clams, all contain symbiotic algal-like organisms called zooxanthellae. These zooxanthellae appear to pay their way by producing oxygen for their host when exposed to light, as well as producing substances on which their host can feed. Important aspects of lighting for these invertebrates are:

Daylength Most coral reefs, with the possible exception of those in the Red Sea, are equatorial, so marine tanks containing invertebrates should have 12–14 hours of daylight.

Intensity Equatorial sun is very bright, so these invertebrates should have a minimum light intensity of 12,000–18,000 lux. (Lux is a unit of illumination equivalent to one lumen per square meter. As a

guide, a 150-watt metal halide lamp suitable for a reef aquarium produces about 10,000 lux.)

Spectrum

Light in the blue end of the spectrum is important for these invertebrates, because the zooxanthellae can use light only within this section. There should be strong peaks in the wavelengths around 425 and 650 nm (nanometers). You can buy separate so-called actinic fluorescent tubes to provide this blue light.

Above: A battery of different lights may be necessary to produce the correct quality of lighting for some marine tanks. This fitting has a high-intensity metal halide lamp and two pairs of actinic and bright white fluorescent tubes.

Below: Light of the correct spectrum, intensity and daylength is essential for the long-term health of many invertebrates, such as these soft and hard corals and anemones, as well as for the algae that the tang grazes on.

TROPICAL MARINE FISH – Behavioral abnormalities

Main sign	Other signs	Species affected	Possible diagnoses	Treatments
Sudden darting movements	Loss of balance, rapid respiration	All	Sudden onset water poisoning; new tank syndrome	Address water quality problem
Blindness		Nocturnal species, especially lionfish (Pterois spp.)	Excessive exposure to bright light.	Reduce lighting levels. Supplement with vitamin A.
Lethargy	Weight loss, excessive mucus production, loss of balance, and death	Angelfish	Angelfish encephalitis virus	None
Respiratory distress	Clamped fins, scratching, and flashing, inactivity	All	Gill flukes	Brand name ectoparasitic preparations. Also praziquantel at 10 mg/liter for a three-hour bath, freshwater dips five minutes for five days
	Irritation, ulceration	All	Brooklynella and Uronema (protozoa)	Copper-based ectoparasitic treatments
Scratching and irritation	Gray skin from excess mucus, reddened skin, ulceration	All	Skin flukes	As for gill flukes
Weakness	Wasting and anemia	All	Hemoparasites (protozoa found in the blood)	Methylene blue at 100 mg/liter for a 24-hour bath, or metronidazole at 50 mg/liter.
Sudden death	Anorexia, lethargy, abdominal fluid accumulation	All	Pancreatic necrosis virus	No treatment
Loss of balance		Male seahorses	Seahorse gas bubble disease	Release air from brood pouch

TROPICAL MARINE INVERTEBRATES – Diseases and disorders

Main sign	Other signs	Species affected	Possible diagnoses	Treatments
Molting difficulties	Reduced activity	Crustaceans	Iodine deficiency	Add brand name trace element supplement that includes iodine.
Soft shells	Deformities, poor growth, death	Crustaceans, mollusks, hard corals	Low levels of dissolved calcium, low pH	Supplement with calcium. Adjust pH.
Bleaching	Death	Corals	Excessively high temperatures triggering loss of zooxanthellae	None – keep in optimum water conditions and hope zooxanthellae reestablish.
Rotting areas	Deterioration and death	Hard and soft corals, anemones	Bacterial infection – often following damage to holdfast	Try antibiotics in water – poor outlook. Consider culling to reduce risk of transmission.
Ulceration	Loss of appetite, death	Octopus species	Bacterial infection	Antibiotics. Poor outlook.
Loss of balance	Usually after being lifted from water	Echinoderms such as sea urchins and starfish	Air trapped in body cavity	Difficult – try dislodging bubble; never take out of the water.
Deterioration	Death	All invertebrates	Copper toxicosis from copper antiparasitic compounds; exposure to copper-treated rocks, coral sand, etc.	Remove invertebrates from the system.
	Reduced activity, death	All invertebrates	Poor water quality – check especially ammonium, nitrite, nitrate, and phosphate levels.	Address water quality problems.
	Shrinking, change of color (shown left)	Corals, anemones, *Tridacna* clams	Insufficient light levels or wrong lighting spectrum	Correct lighting.

TROPICAL MARINE FISH – *Physical abnormalities*

Main sign	Other signs	Species affected	Possible diagnoses	Treatments
Hemorrhages, ulceration	Abnormal swimming, shimmying	All	Bacterial disease	Antibiotics required. Large ulcers may need packing to seal the breach in the osmotic barrier.
Fine white "dusting" on skin	Labored breathing, flashing	All	Coral fish disease (*Amyloodinium*)	Copper-based ectoparasitic treatments
Large discrete white spots			Marine white spot (*Cryptocaryon irritans*)	Copper-based ectoparasitic treatment
Weight loss	Poor growth, swollen abdomen	All	Tapeworms	Praziquantel at 10 mg/liter for a three-hour bath
	Spinal curvature, ulceration	All	Fish tuberculosis (*Mycobacteria*)	Antibiotic treatment not very effective. Consider euthanasia, especially because of the zoonotic risk.
	Thickened areas of inflammation, ulceration, finrot	All	*Nocardia* (Bacterium that causes TB-like signs)	As above
Erosions of muscles at head and along lateral line	Slimy feces	Angelfish and tangs	Head-and-lateral-line disease (Lack of vitamin A). Protozoa/virus infection.	Try vitamin A supplement. Metronidazole at 50 mg/liter daily for 10 days.
Cauliflowerlike growths on fins and skin		All	Lymphocystis	No direct cure. Ozone or UV may reduce spread. Will often heal of its own accord in otherwise healthy fish.

Nodules	Darkened coloring, emaciation, abnormal swimming	All	Sporozoa (protozoa)	No known cure
Nonsymmetrical swelling	Ulceration, loss of balance	All	Neoplasia (tumor)	Surgery or euthanasia
Nonulcerative skin masses	Lethargy, disorientation	Especially seahorses	Exophthaliosis (protozoa)	No effective treatment
Fingerprintlike marks on skin		Tangs and surgeonfish	Tang fingerprint disease virus	No treatment available
Ulcers on snout and mouth	Aggression	Pufferfish	Tiger puffer virus	No treatment available
Damage to skin and/or loss of eyes and fins	Secondary bacterial infections	All	Trauma	Antibiotics. Alter and improve management.
Small black spots over body	Cloudy skin, respiratory distress	All	Turbellaria (protozoa)	Formalin bath at 2 ml formalin per liter for up to one hour. Five-minute freshwater bath daily for five days.

Left: Head-and-lateral-line disease in tangs has been associated with a vitamin A deficiency, rather than with the hexamita-like protozoal infestation suspected in freshwater fish.

Right: The white spots on this blue chromis (Chromis cyanea) strongly suggest a diagnosis of Cryptocaryon irritans, a protozoan parasite.

CREDITS

Practical photographs by Geoffrey Rogers © Interpet Publishing.

The publishers would like to thank the following photographers for providing images, credited here by page number and position: B(Bottom), T(Top), C(Center), BL(Bottom Left), etc.

Aqua Press (M-P & C Piednoir): 6, 26(TR), 44, 49(BR), 52, 59(BC), 6(BL,BR), 7(TR,B) Mary Bailey: 38(B), 42(R), 54(BL,TR) Dave Bevan: 12(BR), 17(TR), 34(TR), 38(T), 41(B), 43(B), 45(BR), 57(BL), 64, 67(BR) David Bucke: 4, 20(C, BC), 41(TR), 42(B), 43(B), 46(T) Peter Burgess: 46(B), 56 Derek Cattani: 39(L) John Glover: 47 S McMahon: 45(TR) Arend van den Nieuwenhuizen: 13(TR), 14(T), 30(B), 34(B), 35(BR) Photomax (Max Gibbs): Title page. 12(T), 14(BL), 15(TL, BC), 19(T), 35(L), 40(R), 43(T), 57(BR), 59(TL, BR) 68, 73, 75(R, L) Mike Sandford: 15(R), 24, 25(TR), 40(B), 41(TC), 45(L) Sue Scott: 26(BR) Iggy Tavares: 17(TC) W A Tomey: 30(TR), 39(BR) William Wildgoose: 20, 67(CL, BC).

Illustrations by Phil Holmes and Stuart Watkinson © Interpet Publishing.

The publishers would like to thank Mary Bailey, Peter Burgess; Heaver Tropics, Ash, Kent and Wey Exotics, Farnham, Surrey for their help.

The information and recommendations in this book are given without any guarantees on the part of the author and publisher, who disclaim any liability with the use of this material.